T0305486

Integrated Reporting Management

Analysis and Applications for Creating Value

Integrated Reporting Management

Analysis and Applications
for Creating Value

Sean Stein Smith

CRC Press
Taylor & Francis Group
Boca Raton London New York

CRC Press is an imprint of the
Taylor & Francis Group, an **informa** business

A PRODUCTIVITY PRESS BOOK

CRC Press
Taylor & Francis Group
6000 Broken Sound Parkway NW, Suite 300
Boca Raton, FL 33487-2742

First issued in paperback 2021

ISBN-13: 978-1-138-49885-3 (hbk)
ISBN-13: 978-1-03-217853-0 (pbk)
DOI: 10.4324/9781351015479

Library of Congress Cataloging-in-Publication Data

Names: Stein Smith, Sean, author.
Title: Integrated reporting management : analysis and applications for creating value / Sean Stein Smith.
Description: 1 Edition. | New York : Taylor & Francis, [2018] | Includes bibliographical references and index.
Identifiers: LCCN 2018027263 (print) | LCCN 2018043807 (ebook) | ISBN 9781351015479 (e-Book) | ISBN 9781138498853 (hardback : alk. paper)
Subjects: LCSH: Communication in organizations. | Organizational behavior.
Classification: LCC HD30.3 (ebook) | LCC HD30.3 .S754 2018 (print) | DDC 651.7/8--dc23
LC record available at https://lccn.loc.gov/2018027263

Visit the Taylor & Francis Web site at
http://www.taylorandfrancis.com

and the CRC Press Web site at
http://www.crcpress.com

This book is dedicated to my family, who have always lent me their support and encouragement along my academic, professional, and personal journey.

Contents

Preface

Financial information and data are the lifeblood that drives the business decision-making process, and even though there are certainly differences and peculiarities unique to every profession, several common themes emerge upon review. First, the data used to plan, evaluate, and track different projects and initiatives must be available in a format that is consistent, comparable, timely, and relevant. If these characteristics sound very similar to the traits that define high quality accounting information, it is not an accident. For better or worse, accounting and financial information represent the language through which businesses are evaluated, and how the individuals tasked with running these organizations are judged. Second, in a globalized business landscape increasingly concerned with how financial results are achieved there is evidence of significant friction between organizations in the marketplace. Specifically, even as media and market analysts dissect and report quarterly financial results, there is an emerging and growing trend toward managing for the medium to long term.

Such tension and conflict between the different stakeholder groups to which management professionals answer creates an environment very different, yet increasingly evident, to the one readily visible to any market analyst. For example, and elaborated throughout this book, is the following reality. Large institutional investors, including but not limited to sovereign wealth funds, pension plan assets, and university endowments, are simultaneously interested in achieved satisfactory financial performance while also facing pressure to divest holdings aligned with non-environmentally friendly businesses. This pull and push are evident in virtually every large investment plan, with management professionals caught between increasing societal pressure and expectations of the marketplace. While some stakeholder groups, including large financial institutions and shareholders, continue to advocate for a longer-term focus and orientation, quarterly earnings reports and analyses continue to dominate the conversation. Bridging this gap, and specifically doing so on a continuous basis, represents both a challenge and opportunity for organizations across industry lines. This connects to a general theme, which dominates the financial reporting conversation: the utilization of consistent reporting standards. Even as management teams seek to, in many cases, balance the expectations of stakeholders with longer-term perspectives and those focused on short-term results, a lack of standardization and consistency poses a substantial issue.

Numerous frameworks, guidelines, and reporting advice exist in the marketplace; the difficulty faced by organizations is not in any way caused by a lack of options. Rather, the fact that so many different options do exist points to a fundamental issue in the realm of organizational reporting. Even though, and this is stated with a high level of confidence, the majority of organizations and management personnel acknowledge the importance of more comprehensive reporting, it continues to be a challenge to transform this interest into action. Integrated reporting, outlined in this book, supported by examples and general context, and connected to broader technology trends, looks like a viable option to help address this multitude of needs the marketplace has generated.

My interest in integrated reporting, as both a CPA practitioner and academic researcher, sprang out of my doctoral research as I sought to bridge the gap between accounting information and a more holistic view of how an organization is performing. While quantitative accounting information may be the language of business, the inclusion of nonfinancial and other operational data provides end users with the context and narrative so necessary for true understanding. What this book will hopefully accomplish, from both a practical and research perspective is to illustrate the potential of integrated reporting, highlight current examples and applications underway, and demonstrate just how powerful this framework can be when connected to other forces already underway in the business landscape.

Sean Stein Smith

Introduction

As of this writing, the global business landscape is becoming increasingly competitive, digitized in nature, and influenced by a wide range of stakeholder groups, including both financial and nonfinancial stakeholders. Documenting, reporting, and analyzing the various streams of information already produced by an organization are tasks that are becoming increasingly not optional, and requires a methodology that can mean the difference between long-term success and an overt emphasis on short-term results. Information and different types of data are what ultimately drive the financial performance of an organization, regardless of the specific industry or geographic region that an organization operates within. Although the reality that information is the proverbial secret sauce driving operational and financial performance is clear, quantifying, reporting, and explaining the value of this information continues to represent a challenge for organizational decision-making.

While it is true that accounting professionals and management teams on a broader basis are tasked with leading and navigating this rapidly evolving business landscape, current reporting standards are not equipped to handle these different flows of information. Traditional financial reporting, for all of the value and information it serves and provides to the marketplace, is limited in both scope and usefulness. Financial reporting, almost without exception, is nearly always prepared for a narrow subset of end users, namely creditors and equity shareholders. Both groups, clearly, are influential and powerful in how an organization navigates and evolves in the marketplace, but are increasingly augmented by nonfinancial stakeholder groups. Regulators, environmental groups, consumer advocacy groups, trade associations, and other NGO institutions are of increasing importance to not only how the organization performs, but how reporting decisions are made and updated over time.

Stepping into this gap and potential void in information and communication that exists within the marketplace is the integrated reporting framework and model supported and put forward by the International Integrated Reporting Council (IIRC). While not a cure-all for the woes and shortcomings of current reporting standards and information, an integrated report creates a framework and information that allows financial and nonfinancial streams of information to be reported on equal footing. It is clear there are still gaps in the reporting process and informational procedures that underpin the integrated reporting process at large, but there are several attributes that make integrated reporting superior to existing or past frameworks. Explained and documented throughout this book, including both examples of current implementation and prospects for future adoption, these different characteristics differentiate integrated reporting from other available options.

The focus of this text, including examples, commentaries, and information, serves two purposes for readers. First, the purpose is to explain and frame the argument and narrative around integrated financial reporting, including the importance of stakeholder theory for the implementation and continuation of integrated reporting. Second, and diving into the aspects and technical areas of integrated reporting, including the connection between integrated reporting, technology, and the changing stakeholder landscape, this book analyzes how external trends are influencing the concept of reporting. Additionally, and important for management teams and professionals seeking to adapt an integrated reporting framework, current market examples and resources have been provided for analysis and comparison.

Put simply, this book seeks to address and communicate the core issues and information linked to this rapidly growing area, and equip professionals with the information they need to succeed and adapt to a rapidly changing business environment. Cutting through the hype and buzzwords that all too often surround innovative thinking, ideas, and platforms, this book drills down into specific connections, linkages, and how these ideas link to broader market trends. Written in a conversational tone, this book and the resources it contains will be helpful for practitioners, academics, and anyone looking to gain an edge in the competitive market.

Author

Sean Stein Smith is an assistant professor at Lehman College, City University of New York and is a member of the 2017 AICPA Leadership Academy. He was named a "40 under 40" by *CPA Practice Advisor* (2017). He was also named a Young Professional of the Year by the Institute of Management Accountants (2016) and honored with a "30 under 30" by the NJCPA (2015). Before transitioning to higher education, Dr. Stein Smith worked at the intersection of accounting and technology, specifically focusing on leveraging technology to improve the speed and quality of accounting information. His research and writings about accounting, sustainability initiatives, and the increasing technological integration of the profession have been featured in dozens of academic, practitioner, and media publications. Additionally, Dr. Stein Smith has led CPE sessions and presentations at national and international events, discussing sustainability, technology, and the accounting profession—attracting thousands of attendees. He earned his doctoral degree in 2015, writing on the subject of corporate strategy and how accounting professionals will develop into strategic partners in the face of changing market conditions.

Chapter 1

The Case for a New Type of Reporting

Change is always difficult, and it is even more difficult to plan, implement, and sustain when it pertains to the multifaceted environment facing management teams and organizations. Emphasizing the additional reporting and compliance obligations is not a viable pathway to jump starting this conversation, but it is important that potential stakeholders understand both the components, possible challenges, and the opportunities embedded within the concept of an integrated financial report. Chapter 1 introduces both the idea of integrated reporting and some of the surrounding context, which makes this specific time frame amenable for the adoption of integrated financial reporting. Integrated reporting is a new concept and idea that has recently taken the business landscape by storm, but does build on previous reporting frameworks and conversations. While the specific components of integrated reporting, including the idea of a multiple capital model, represent innovative thinking, the communication of a broader flow of data is not a new idea. What is new, however, and critically important as integrated reporting becomes more mainstream, is that reporting nonfinancial data are becoming standard, versus optional or a nice thing to have (Figure 1.1).

Issues with Traditional Financial Reporting

As the world and business landscape continue to become increasingly competitive, interconnected, and digitized, there are several fundamental truths becoming apparent to the users of organizational data. First, financial shareholders and

1

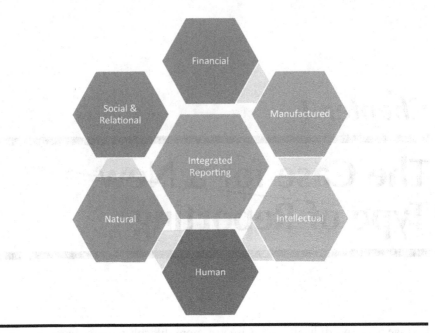

Figure 1.1 Integrated reporting.

nonfinancial stakeholders are increasingly interested in a broader array of operational and organizational data than ever before. This reflects the underlying truth that operational results and information are what ultimately drive the financial performance of organizations, and that by merely focusing on the financial outcomes, analysts and end users only have an incomplete view of the organization. Second, traditional financial reporting, in addition to ignoring much of the operational and organizational information that drive financial performance, takes several months to prepare and disseminate to external users of information. Put simply, traditional and current financial reporting is simply insufficient when trying to fulfill the expectations of stakeholder groups, both internal and external to the organization. Adding to this complexity is the fact that preparing and auditing financial statements can take months and is not currently completed on a continuous basis. Figure 1.2 illustrates, albeit simplistically, the forces often obliging management teams to choose between decisions made for one end-user group versus another, with the associated ripple effects driving the organization forward.

This lag, which for larger corporations can be as long as 6 months, is attributed both to how financials are produced and to the underlying technology systems in place to facilitate this reporting. In a business landscape where markets can move dramatically in a span of several hours, and where information moves at the speed of a click, having to wait several months for financial information is simply unsustainable. Last, but arguably most important, traditional reporting

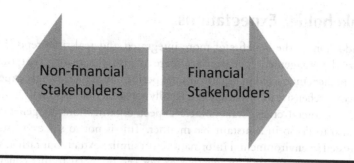

Figure 1.2 Stakeholders versus shareholders.

documents and processes only appeal to a relatively narrow set of end users, most commonly shareholders and creditors. Clearly, this is rooted in a logical perspective, as shareholders and creditors provide the capital and market support for management to pursue certain objectives and plans. This clarity aside, however, it is apparent that interested users include a far broader audience that just shareholders and creditors.

Viewed in this broader context, the issues and concerns that routinely affect the auditing and reporting process are merely the tip of the proverbial iceberg. Stakeholders, both financial and nonfinancial in nature, increasingly expect information to be reported in a continuous manner, and to also reflect the current status of the organization. Traditional financial reporting, as it is currently constituted, simply will not fulfill the expectations and requirements of stakeholders moving forward. Prior to delving into the expectations of stakeholders in a globalized business environment, it is imperative to highlight some of the other issues and topics driving the dissatisfaction with the status quo as it relates to reporting information to the marketplace. Unfortunately, the issues and gap between market expectations and reporting information are not only linked to the specific information embedded within the reporting framework, but also the impact current reporting has on stakeholder engagement.

Traditional reporting, in addition to the time lag and delay between when the transaction occurs versus when the information is reported, is also a process that occurs periodically. Even for the largest corporations, which have quarterly or other periodic reporting requirements, these reports are usually only filed on a monthly or quarterly basis, which leads to the reality that only some information is analyzed and sifted through on a continuous basis. With ever larger amounts of information and data flowing in and out of organizations, simply examining data on a quarterly basis, for example, would appear to be insufficient in the current marketplace and ultimately lead to subpar decision-making. The argument can be made that, in such an environment, information and the ability to effectively leverage this information form the core of new competitive advantages in the global business landscape moving forward.

Stakeholder Expectations

In addition to the benefits of more integrated and real-time reporting, from an internal management perspective, there is also the reality that the variety of stakeholders interested in organizational performance increasingly expect real-time and comprehensive information. It is readily apparent that, especially in the aftermath of the financial crisis, stakeholders expect organizations to generate earnings, but also to do so in a sustainable manner. This is not to say every stakeholder is interested in environmental information to a similar extent, but rather, stakeholders are increasingly focused on whether or not the financial results generated by the organization will be sustained in the medium to long term. Linking directly to this requirement (where organizations create value and financial performance on a consistent basis) is the concept and idea that management professionals should shift from a quarterly basis of financial performance to a longer-term perspective.

This shift in perception and evaluative tactics, however, is nothing new, innovative, nor a recent iteration based on feedback from the financial crisis; it is something that may even seem intuitive for stakeholder groups and users of organizational information. That said, it is important to recognize that while these facts and understandings of organizational performance may seem like common sense, they are not in alignment with many management practices, nor with the methods by which organizations are routinely evaluated. Taking this into account, the differentiation between how management professionals should generate value and lead the organization internally, and what external tools should be used presents both a challenge and opportunity. A fundamental challenge, framed within the context of current financial reporting, is that even though management professionals need to develop talent, products, and services to sustain growth, such an approach may lead to lower short-term returns in the present.

While the prerogative of management is, in the strictest sense, to maximize shareholder value, the specific ways in which this value is maximized has become an even livelier topic of debate since 2007–2008. In essence, and using as reference the number of organizations that suffered negative consequences as a result of placing short-term results ahead of longer term performance, there appears to be a trend in the market toward generating value in both the short and longer term. This is not merely a minor concern, or an item only being brought to the attention of management by a small subset of stakeholders; rather, it is one of the highest priority items on the management list of many large institutional shareholders. Specifically, there are trillions of dollars in assets invested in a variety of environmental, social, and governance (ESG) indices, which is as clear as any indicator that these issues are gaining increasing amounts of attention. Such financial commitment and allocation of resources represents a clear and unequivocal indication of the importance being placed on sustainability and nonfinancial data from both an operational and financial perspective.

Such an increased interest in environmental, social, and governance items is, of course, a matter related to the bottom line, but is also an indicator and trend linked directly to stakeholder expectations. Taking a step back and viewing this from a longer-term perspective, it is important to acknowledge just what types of organizations and institutions are part of this stakeholder community. While stakeholders and financial shareholders are both interested in how the organization performs from a financial perspective, the stakeholder environment is also comprised of a large number of organizations that have different goals and objectives. Financial resources are not exclusively allocated to financial institutions and shareholders; an increasing variety of institutions include pensions, endowments, and other nongovernmental organizations have assets invested with assets managers. These assets, and the multiple objectives associated with these investments, also produce a situation in which financial and non-financial returns must be balanced. While financial performance is, of course, important for the management professionals of these different institutions, there are other concerns arguably equally as important.

Expectations and objectives from the perspective of stakeholder management include the reality that, in addition to achieving short-term financial objectives, the organizations which are the focus of investment funds must also generate sustainable returns over medium and long-term periods of time. The ability of a management team to consistently deliver satisfactory returns, from a financial and operational perspective, allows the stakeholders making investments to fund their individual objectives while also satisfying fiduciary responsibilities in relation to contributed funds. The increasing influence of stakeholders, both from an investment point of view and how organizations engage with the marketplace at large, is also linked to a growing trend in how organizations are evaluated. Simply achieving short-term (quarterly or otherwise) financial results is not enough to generate value in a marketplace focused on a more holistic and comprehensive view of organizational performance.

Tying in Integrated Reporting

There is no one clear-cut answer, no panacea, and no proverbial silver bullet to address the multifaceted and complex issues facing management teams, organizations, and stakeholders in a business environment that requires a larger variety of information. Integrated financial reporting, although offering no guaranteed solution to assist with these issues, does provide a platform from which management can conduct these conversations and enact appropriate changes. A fundamental flaw in many of the current reports linked to ESG data and information is a lack of consistent and comparable information. Many different platforms and reporting tools are available in the marketplace, including other competing frameworks linked to sustainability of information; however, with the number of options available there is also a possibility that some information is overlooked, misreported, or not reported in a comparable manner from one period to the next.

Simply acknowledging the fact that there is significant pressure on management teams and professionals to create value over the medium and long term, however, is not a business case or business plan. When a management concept or idea is introduced, regardless of how this specific idea will influence and drive management decision-making, it must be supported by business benefits. Reporting, compliance, and other back-office activities are already time consuming and resource draining activities for organizations, so layering on additional compliance requirements will not be met with enthusiasm across industry lines. In order to succeed, and achieve broader adoption and implementation, there must be a direct linkage and connection between integrated reporting and the performance of organizations. If this connection is not evident, or cannot be explained and reported to different stakeholder groups, this initiative and concept will simply not succeed.

Of course, and specifically when it comes to analyzing the ripple effects of integrated reporting in the broader marketplace, it may be difficult to establish correlation or causality. In other words, are the organizations that have implemented integrated reporting to date succeeded because of this implementation or were they able to adopt a more robust reporting framework due to financial success and resources? It is beyond the scope of this research and book to provide a definitive answer on this subject, primarily because this area and its implementation are still relatively nascent in nature. What this research and book hopes to provide, rather, is a comprehensive review and analysis of both current trends in integrated reporting. Included in such an analysis is an introduction to the topic, a review of underlying trends and support for this framework, as well as analyses of market leaders currently using integrated reporting in the marketplace.

An important point that should be emphasized when conducting an analysis of integrated financial reporting, especially versus current existing options and frameworks, is that several characteristics differentiate integrated reporting framework from other options. First, and perhaps most important to the growing conversation around the importance of organizational information, is the multiple capital model embedded within the integrated reporting framework. Creating a framework to consistently and effectively report different types of information and data, both for internal and external users, may very well be how organizations succeed and indeed thrive in the global marketplace moving forward. The specific framework and information framework embedded within integrated reporting sets this framework apart from other options in the marketplace.

Fundamental characteristics of quality information, whether represented from an ESG, operational, or financial perspective, is that the information must be consistent, comparable, timely, and relevant to the decision-making process. Consistent and comparable information, regardless of what the specific types of information are, forms the basis for how decisions are made, including the metrics often used to track the performance of the firm over the medium and long term. Integrated reporting, through the establishment of multiple types of capital, and development of a consistent framework through which information can communicate different types of data allows accountants and management professionals to leverage the increased available information. Analyzing and reporting these different streams of information also links directly to the importance of long-term value creation from an organization perspective. In order to create and generate value in a short-term and longer-term perspective.

Long-Term Value Case

Creating and sustaining value over the long term is something that, in addition to fulfilling quarterly and other period earnings goals, is a fiduciary responsibility of any management team. Many of the most successful organizations currently in the marketplace, including market leaders such as Amazon and Starbucks, employ a management philosophy focused on both the current bottom line and methodologies to generate value in the future. While this might, at first glance, appear to be only relevant for larger organizations, the concept of creating value over the long term is a responsibility and prerogative of management teams across industry lines. Understanding that, despite industry affiliation or status as either a "for profit" or "nonprofit" enterprise, that management professionals must maximize resources. Despite differences in industry or other types of management prerogatives, the underlying goal of management is to create and generate assets in excess of the debts and liabilities required to generate these assets.

Long-term value creation, from a business analysis perspective, seems to make perfectly logical sense from both an internal and external perspective, but the reality on the ground is much more complicated. Shareholders, including analysts employed by financial institutions and the larger investors, place extraordinary amounts of pressure on organizations to successfully achieve—and often exceed—projected financial results. Reporting information on a quarterly or other short-term periodic basis has a contradictory effect on the case for sustainable long-term value creation and management. This emphasis, driven by financial shareholders and creditors, is a logical and expected point of view from individuals and organizations whose primary interest is in achieving a reasonable rate of return. Unfortunately, this emphasis on short-term results and information is not merely an academic or theoretical problem, and can have a crippling effect on the long-term success of the organization.

On a global basis, the total amount of financial resources dedicated to share repurchases and buybacks total trillions of dollars, which has assisted in increasing returns for shareholders. Repurchasing shares may boost short-term financial performance, and satisfy some of the stakeholders interested in the performance of the organization, but it does not create an environment where long-term investment, or product development, is prioritized. Viewed in this narrow context, the returns and benefits of these behaviors have benefitted the most traditionally important group of an organization—financial shareholders. Taking a step back, and viewing this behavior in the context of broader business issues, and the imperative to generate value in a sustainable manner, these actions do not appear to represent the most efficient use of organizational resources. Much has been written and discussed about the value and business case for share repurchases and buyback activity, but one fundamental fact remains unchanged. In order to fund these repurchases and buybacks, funds allocated to these activities are not available for other investments and issues.

In the landscape of historically low interest rates, the need to raise additional capital from either investors or creditors might seem to be a minor inconvenience for management, but the reality is not that simple. Underinvesting in capital assets, cutting back on training and development programs, and focusing the expertise of management purely on cost reduction are simply not activities leading to sustainable growth over the medium and long-term. These are not new facts, and this is not a new conversation in the marketplace between analysts, users of financial information, and other stakeholders. What has traditionally been lacking, however, is the ability of management to use nonfinancial information in a consistent and continuous manner. Simply discussing these issues on a periodic basis is insufficient, and must be accompanied by an action plan, investments, and the dedication of management to address these issues. What is necessary, particularly in an era of global uncertainty and increasing global competition, is an action-oriented framework.

Pressure from Shareholders

An action-oriented plan, however, is not something that can be created in vacuum or without substantial input and tweaking from financial shareholders and other external stakeholder groups. Put simply, and acknowledging the fact that nonfinancial stakeholders are beginning to exercise more influence over the decision-making process, the leverage and influence brought to bear by financial stakeholders is substantial. Larry Fink, the founder and CEO of Blackrock, one of the largest asset managers in the world with over $6 trillion under management, appears to be one of the most high-profile ambassadors and leaders of this sea change. Recognizing the reality that it is virtually impossible for corporations to consistently achieve superior financial performance without being an engaged member of the broader community forms the basis of this most recent initiative. While some others in the financial services industry, and broader community at large have expressed doubt as to the validity of these overtures, the trend they highlight cannot be ignored.

Financial shareholders, whether they represent institutional or individual shareholders, in addition to representing the most active constituents in virtually every instance, also represent the constituents most likely to push for change. Harnessing this interest and capacity to drive change throughout the organization is another opportunity that may initially appear as a challenge to the organization. Since financial shareholders, analysts, and investment professionals are most likely to influence not only how the organization is managed, but what projects and ideas are funded, appealing to common interests in alignment with the shareholders' goals appears to be a logical place to start. That said, and once again highlighting the difference between integrated reporting and other nonfinancial reporting frameworks is the fact that although the multiple capital model (MCM) resembles current reporting standards and frameworks, there are substantial differences.

Investment managers and management professionals in various organizations have a variety of fiduciary duties and responsibilities they must enforce and abide by. First, the actions undertaken by the management team and organization must be in the best interest of financial shareholders, at least in as much as the fiduciary duty is often currently interpreted. By placing financial shareholders—specifically the interests of equity holders above all others, it is all too possible to see long-term investments put on the proverbial back burner. Second, the strategic initiatives underway in the organization must be conducted in an ethical manner in compliance with all applicable laws and regulations. This, however, can be difficult when doing business overseas, or attempting to oversee a supply chain that spans multiple continents and even more numerous legal jurisdictions. Last, but not least, is the expectation and obligation of management professionals to seek growth and business expansion, to both fulfill market expectations and fend off the competition. When this growth and expansion take the form of financial engineering and other machinations, however, the long-term viability of the organization may be put into question.

Figure 1.3 highlights the fact that on top of the intellectual debate that often surrounds this discussion, this conversation involves real world users with real world influence and effects. Management professionals have a fiduciary duty, clearly, to

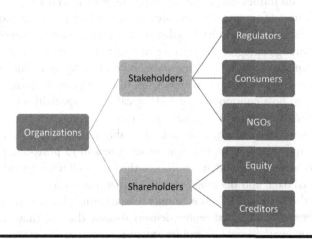

Figure 1.3   Audiences for organizational information and user groups.

maximize returns for shareholders and that is not changing at this point. This being said, it is important to recognize that in addition to this responsibility there is also a growing pressure among organizations and stakeholders to fulfill broader reporting and operational goals. Stakeholders, however, are not simply environmental groups, but can and often do include consumers, regulators, and other governmental partners. While not traditional shareholders, the influence exercised by these groups is not insubstantial.

The Need for an Action-Oriented Plan

Clearly there is an increased interest in the ability of an organization to generate sufficient financial returns not only in the short term but in the medium and long term well; however, interest by itself is not sufficient. Time and again, one of the most consistent flaws in the attempts and frameworks used to collect, quantify, and report different types of nonfinancial information is that these different frameworks and concepts do not generate information on par with what is produced by traditional financial reporting. In order for quantitative information to have worth and value to a management team it must have the following four characteristics: (1) it must be comparable, (2) consistent, (3) relevant, and (4) timely; all of which are embedded within the data reported and disseminated through traditional reporting processes. Attempting to present a more comprehensive view of organizational performance, however, requires that organizations adopt a more comprehensive approach to reporting information. In short, in order to effectively transition from a traditional—exclusively financial and historical—reporting process to one that is inclusive, forward looking, and comprehensive in nature, a new type of plan and framework is necessary. Specifically, the need and market expectation of an action-oriented plan and framework, consistent with traditional reporting, is evident.

Taking action, of course, virtually always sounds like a recommended scenario or plan to initiate, lead, and sustain effective business change; however, the reality is that even though integrated reporting may appear to represent a step forward in the marketplace, adoption will inevitably take time. Approaching the adoption and implementation of integrated reporting, like any other large-scale project or idea, appears to be a common sense and logical idea, especially since in order to it effectively it requires both internal and external changes to the organization. Rolling out new ideas and processes will inevitably cause difficulty and encounter obstacles during this process, but that is not a reason to postpone this process. Rather, abundant market evidence points to the increased interest and importance of nonfinancial data, and the longevity this shift seems to offer.

Some of the key considerations to take into account when analyzing the value and possibilities an integrated report delivers include the fact that the integrated reporting framework closely resembles existing reporting structures. In essence, what an integrated reporting process does is attempt to leverage and maximize the existing competencies of accounting professionals to more effectively report on broader varieties of information. Changing and altering the status quo of financial and public market reporting is no small task, nor is it a task that can be completed in one cycle. A critical part of this process, shifting from exclusively focusing on short-term financial results to longer-term operational and financial information, is the ability of management to convince external users of the validity of this shift. While some organizations, including those in the International Integrated Reporting Council (IIRC) reporting database, have already begun the process of reporting data to the market on a less frequent basis, this process requires management to have a business case for this change and shift in reporting priorities. Although reporting different types of information and data to external users may attract most of the focus and scrutiny, that is, the graphics, charts, and other information that is distributed may receive most of the commentary, there are other important changes that must also take place. Stated another way, even though the majority of information communicated has traditionally been financial in nature, other underlying and operational information must also be distributed on an ongoing basis.

Generating an impetus to take action to get this process underway, and to provide management with the sure footing required to explain and justify these shifts and changes, is imperative for the adoption of a more integrated reporting framework. Integrated reporting aligned with the very nature of the reporting process itself, necessitates several changes internally at the organizational level to be effective. In this context, where management professionals are often in a conflict between financial market forces and the expectations of broader stakeholder management teams there is a need for action. That said, and again going back to the need for consistency and standardization related to different types of information, a framework and reporting structure provides an appropriate vehicle for delivering this data to external users. Taking a step back, it is obvious there are a number of different frameworks and options available to organizations and management teams; therefore, what is the differentiating value proposition of integrated reporting? Like any other template, framework, or business initiative or idea, there has to be a value-added proposition to facilitate the adoption of this framework. Discussing the context driving the implementation and adoption of integrated reporting—specifically stakeholder reporting—provides the much needed information for professionals seeking to learn more about integrated reporting.

Stakeholder Theory

Underpinning the need and desire for an integrated report is the reality that in an increasingly globalized environment and business landscape the needs and expectations of stakeholder groups continue to evolve. The necessity for a robust and comprehensive reporting framework is readily apparent regardless of what industry a specific organization operates within. Financial shareholders are clearly powerful and influential members of the stakeholder community, but a broader approach is required. At the essence of the idea, stakeholder theory necessitates that the organization takes into account the needs and expectations of other end users of organizational data. Such an approach may seem unnecessary or perhaps idealistic when facing the requirement of the financial markets, but that would be an incomplete view of the current situation. Stakeholders, including both financial and nonfinancial stakeholders, form a core constituency for management professionals to engage with on a continuous basis. Clearly, financial markets and providers of credit and capital exercise influence and have insights applicable to management decision-making, but the growing influence of nonfinancial stakeholders continues to increase in an increasingly digitized and globalized environment.

Reiterated throughout this text, and demonstrated in Figure 1.4, is the reality that even though this conversation is not necessarily a new one, the current representation and focus toward reporting and information communication tends to be weighted toward financial reporting, which again makes sense given the current market construct. This preferential treatment of shareholder needs and requirements is a well-known fact in financial markets and among reporting entities, regardless of geographic location of industry affiliation. That said, there does appear to be, and it can take the form of benefit corporations, integrated reporting, or other comprehensive reporting frameworks, and definitive market demand for more comprehensive and holistic reporting of information to end users. Simply put, the imbalance and issues linked to this imbalance do appear to be recognized broadly by market participants.

Acknowledging this situation, however, is merely the first step toward the creation of a more dynamic and engaging dialogue between organizations and applicable stakeholder groups. Communicating information, engaging in productive conversations, and using this dialogue to facilitate a more robust strategic plan

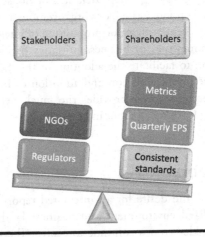

Figure 1.4 Current representation of influence mismatch over reporting.

require several other factors. First, different end users of organizational data will expect, and in some instances require, different types of information focusing on different aspects of organizational performance. Differentiating these different types of data, and assessing the internal capabilities of the organization to produce this information is a logical first step to begin this analysis. This may result in not only a different presentation of information, including graphics and other sorts of illustrative tools, but often will require different streams of information. Stakeholders will vary from organization to organization, and the types of information will be different, but these trends remain unchanged.

Second, after identifying and analyzing which types of information are necessary to deliver to different stakeholder groups, an internal assessment must be conducted. This aspect, the internal review and assessment of information availability, is where many management teams may face difficulty. While an abundance of information is available within organizations, with more becoming available virtually everyday due to technological advances, analyzing these vast amounts of data remains a work in progress. Implementing the Internet of things (IoT), for example, provides management with vast amounts of information, which would appear to facilitate the implementation of an increasingly stakeholder-oriented reporting methodology. With different types of information becoming available, and this information being connected to an array of operations of activities within the organization, management teams will have virtually every type of data required for comprehensive reporting. Reporting this information, however, remains a challenge for the following reason—a robust capital framework remains a work in progress. Integrated reporting, while not representing a panacea for organizations nor an idea that will change the business fundamentals of the organization, does appear to facilitate the reporting and communication of information.

Stakeholder Theory in a Globalized World

Stakeholder theory may appear to be a theoretical idea, or a concept best left to an academic debate of think tank professionals, but the underlying business case and reality is that stakeholder groups have a tremendous impact on business performance and engagement. While financial markets and investors are most interested in the success and performance of the organization, there is a substantial percentage of market funding and stakeholders interested in both financial returns and areas of importance. Consumers around the globe are interested not only in how the organization generates profits and financial performance, but if those profits and earnings are created in a way conducive to the requirements and expectations of consumer groups. Also important for industries seeking to capitalize on emerging areas of economic importance and influence, is the impact of regulatory and NGO institutions on how management makes decisions from a qualitative perspective, and from a capital allocation point of view.

Capital allocation is a core fiduciary responsibility of management professionals and has traditionally been viewed through a relatively narrow lens and perspective. Put simply, every dollar of financial capital invested in a strategic initiative or project must be able to generate sufficient returns to validate these activities irrespective of other actions or activities. This may appear to be a reasonable and logical evaluative methodology for financial capital, but this only focuses on a narrow set of end users. Creditors, interested in the ability of an organization to generate sufficient cash flows to cover interest and applicable principal payments, represent a traditional stakeholder group focused exclusively on financial performance. Investors and equity shareholders, in a related methodology and using criteria similar to creditor groups, are interested in two distinct measures and metrics of performance. Namely, the ability of an organization to generate the current levels of revenue and profits required to drive the capacity of organizations to fund expansion efforts, dividends, and other initiatives (Figure 1.5).

Taking a step back from the quarterly reporting process, however, it is evident that the true driving force behind financial performance, in both the shorter and longer-term context, are the operational results and information generated by different parts of the organization. Organizing these different streams of data, and more importantly taking these flows of data and refining them into dashboards and metrics to facilitate decision-making, is ultimately what enables management professionals to generate and execute effective decisions. While appearing relatively obvious upon initial review, it is also important to take into account the reality that financial performance and metrics may also vary depending on the context of the decision itself. From certain decisions and situations, income and earnings figures may matter more, and in other situations the cash flow performance and projections moving forward may be the deciding factors. This alignment between different sources of information is not a new concept or idea within the financial community, and really this simply represents an extension of existing skills and competencies already in the marketplace.

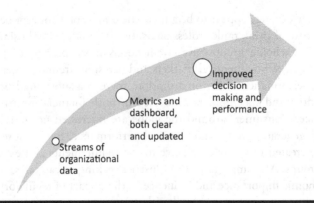

Figure 1.5   Information flows toward improved decision-making.

Additionally, shareholder groups and other equity investors are also interested in the capability of financial investments and projects to generate growth and increase the current levels of profitability and income. Growth and the ability of organizations to consistently generate financial growth form a cornerstone of how management professionals are judged and evaluated by market participants. Specifically, the current stock price of an organization is often connected and directly linked to the projected future cash flows of an organization, without taking into account associated debt or other negative externalities. This lack of comprehensive analysis and presentation forms a shortcoming and gap in both what stakeholder groups expect from organizations in the current globalized environment versus the current reporting standards and frameworks used by market participants. Connecting financial investments and results of organizations represents a need for certain stakeholder groups, and also a method by which management can distinguish their organization from the competition. Data, it is often said, represents the newest resource-driven competitive advantage management professionals have at their disposal, and it links directly to both the digitization of business, and rise of integrated reporting.

Stakeholder Theory in a Digital Age

At the convergence of the stakeholder theory, integrated reporting, and more comprehensive reporting of information overall lies the increased digitization of data, information, and communication methodologies at place within organizations. Specifically, and in addition the proverbial reams of financial data already produced, the advances in digital technology now allows organizations access to vast amounts of operational and other non-financial data. Information is increasingly available in real time, stored in digital format, and is often available via a cloud platform and shared between organizations and supply chain partners. While these advances certainly make information analysis and reporting simpler and more cost effective, it can also create challenges for organizations seeking to effectively gain leverage from this information. Just because information and data are available and readily processed, it does not automatically mean that greater insights will be gained from this information. Processing this information, developing appropriate frameworks and templates, and delivering this information to stakeholders in a timely manner require several changes throughout the organizational process, both internally and externally.

Internal changes necessary to orient the organization toward more comprehensive stakeholder reporting require that both senior management and other employees be well versed in nonfinancial information and terminology. Breaking down the siloes that often exist within organizations is a tactic and strategy that appears to dovetail effectively with the rise and implementation of integrated financial reporting. In essence, integrated reporting and the embedded multiple capital model attempt to provide a quantitative framework for management to use for reporting purposes. While simply announcing a framework and developing several reporting structures will not instantly create a robust reporting framework, it is an important step in the process. Digital information and the speed with which management decisions must be made in a global environment also require that stakeholder consultation should be a component of the business decision-making process. Internal changes and the development of cross-functional teams are important first steps; however, these must be paired with external changes and developments as well.

Every industry is different, and each individual organization is going to be impacted by regulatory changes and forces in different ways, nevertheless it is important to recognize that these external forces are increasingly having an impact on how organizational decisions are made. Whether these stakeholders are most interested in environmental decision-making, operational efficiency and associated information, customer service data, or the sustainability of earnings performance, the underlying implication is the same. In addition to being aware of the pressures and expectations of financial shareholders large and small, stakeholders are increasingly gaining representation at the board and senior management level. Whether by direct representation, or by proxy in the form of large institutional investors, nonfinancial information and data are growing in importance for the decision-making process.

Maintaining effective shareholder and stakeholder relationships is an important fiduciary duty and responsibility, but communicating the changes in the business environment, including a more comprehensive reporting structure, will necessitate an iterative approach and require a transition over time. Making effective decisions—and doing so while utilizing internal and external resources in an effective manner, requires that management teams be not overly occupied in dealing with shareholder concerns. Specifically, activist investors and other possibly distracting shareholder actions can detract and distract management from charting a long-term course for the organization. Even when internal changes have been made to better analyze and report these different flows and types of data, if external stakeholders and shareholders are not on-board with these changes, friction will result. This is another reason why a robust and comprehensive methodology for reporting both financial and nonfinancial data are critical in an increasingly global and stakeholder-oriented business environment.

Connecting Stakeholder Theory to Integrated Reporting

Stakeholder theory and integrated reporting may seem like two completely different areas, especially if reporting is thought of as simply publishing financial information to the marketplace. Conversely, the idea and concept of stakeholder theory may, at least at first glance, appear to be a qualitative framework put together to fulfill the needs and expectations of nonfinancial stakeholders. While this perception may have traditionally been an accurate assessment of what stakeholder theory is, and what stakeholders represented, this perception and definition is in need of an expansion and renewed characterization. The expanding and changing nature of how integrated reporting links to stakeholder theory focuses on two distinct areas and connects to both the ideas of integrated reporting and stakeholders themselves.

Other nonfinancial frameworks and guidelines certainly exist in the marketplace and certainly add value to organizations and management teams who put them into place, but a lack of cohesion between different guidelines, associations, or financial data can lead to confusion and lack of consistency on an organizational basis. Drilling down, and taking into account the different frameworks and findings that can find result from different frameworks, it readily becomes apparent that a more comprehensive option is desirable. For example, and building off market trends already in existence, even simply trying to define and characterize what different non-GAAP metrics represent can cause unnecessary confusion and debate. Although many of these terms, such as cash flow per share and adjusted earnings per share, may already be in use by a number of organizations, attempting to quantify and report nonfinancial data can become even more complicated. Different frameworks, findings, and information will always matter more for some organizations and industries than others, but quantifying and communicating operational information is important regardless of specific businesses.

First, integrated reporting is not simply another reporting framework or compliance requirement designed to be layered onto existing reporting structures and methods. Current reporting, both financial and nonfinancial, already does an adequate job in communicating and publishing certain types of information to the marketplace. Arguably more important, in addition to communicating this information, current reporting structures and frameworks communicate this information in a timely and consistent manner to end users comfortable receiving these types of data. Constructing a template and framework to communicate not only financial data currently reported, but also to include nonfinancial and operational data important to organizational success are a key differentiator in integrated reporting. While it is certainly true that some options do exist, and these current reporting options do result in some consistency and standardization in how nonfinancial data are communicated, gaps still exist.

Focusing on the specifics, the primary causes of the existing gap between what stakeholders expect and what organizations report can be distilled into two primary drivers. First, every organization and every industry is different and will have access to different types of information at certain intervals. Financial information, be it net income, assets, or cash flow, is the same across industry and geographic lines, with currency issues also able to be resolved using standard translation or remeasurement techniques. Nonfinancial data, be it information linked to environmental initiatives, customer feedback and survey information, or data connected to employee training and development are not treated, measured, or reported in a consistent framework in the majority of situations. Rather, and what is often cited as the primary shortcoming of nonfinancial reporting, is that these types of information are reported in a haphazard, inconsistent, or otherwise unuseful manner.

Second, and indicative of the importance that financial shareholders play in how organizations are led and managed, is a perception that nonfinancial stakeholders are not as high profile or as influential as financial shareholders. This perception, however, is not entirely accurate, especially in a globalized business environment that increasingly drives growth and innovation across industry lines. Addressing these issues—including the reality that by doing business across geographic and industry lines organizations will inevitably have to answer to multiple stakeholder groups—has the potential to fundamentally change the reporting landscape. Interestingly, stakeholders also increasingly include financial parties and intermediaries as well as nonfinancial organizations, which may make this transition less dramatic than previously forecasted.

These two forces, which are augmented by the increased integration of technology throughout the business management process, create a business environment virtually tailor-made for the adoption of a more comprehensive reporting framework. Information drives the decision-making process within every organization, but it is important for management professionals employed therein to harness the sheer volume of data already produced by various systems and processes within the firm. Integrated reporting, complete with the embedded multiple capital model, presents managers with a quantitative framework, complete with reports and quantifying metrics similar to how financial data are currently distributed to end users. Technology is of course an overarching theme and trend within the broader business environment, and can lend particularly powerful assistance to the reporting process, especially since data are produced on a nearly continuous basis.

Chapter 2

Why Integrated Reporting

With the wide array and variety of options available for management teams to quantify and report nonfinancial and operational data there is a logical question that must be addressed. Put simply, with the numerous options, frameworks, and reporting tools that exist in the marketplace, why is it assumed integrated reporting is superior to existing and alternative reporting structures. This chapter outlines and analyzes not only some of the aspects of integrated financial reporting, including which specific attributes are included therein, but also what benefits these attributes can deliver to the marketplace. Communicating these benefits and values associated with an integrated report is critical to facilitating its adoption, especially as organizations are already dealing with numerous reporting and compliance requirements. This process also highlights one of the other ideas that should be a part of any conversation around integrated reporting—the business case and value proposition. If it is important for any other business project, it should be included in this conversation as well.

How Integrated Reporting Developed

The history and track record of nonfinancial reporting is a long and well-traveled path many organizations, professional associations, and stakeholders have followed previously. From the 1960s to the increased interest in sustainability during the 1970s, coinciding with the passage of numerous environmental regulations, the interest in operating in an environmentally friendly and sustainable manner is not a recent development. This increased interest, and the myriad of different stakeholder groups invested in these sustainability efforts, led to an equally varied number of proposed ideas and solutions on how to quantify and report these data. Compounding this issue was the reality that, in addition to professional standards and frameworks, individual organizations report different amounts of types of data. Solving these issues is not a simple task, but integrated reporting has shown promise in this direction.

An important theme to keep in mind with the analysis of integrated reporting is that while it is at its core a reporting framework, it is also much more than just another way to report information. Taking into account the different flows of information and data produced also enables management professionals to examine how these influence the decision-making process. Such an approach also provides additional opportunities for management to improve internal and external performance. Simply by focusing on, and paying attention to, the variety of information already being produced by the organization frees up mindshare and expertise for gleaning different insights to evaluate options, and develop new ideas and tactics for future growth. Charting a path forward, and developing a business plan able to survive the ups and downs of the marketplace requires that management be able to judge, evaluate, and utilize the various streams of information available.

It is also important to note that integrated reporting, in addition to appealing to a stakeholder community that includes nonfinancial stakeholders, also seems to appeal and work for financial shareholders and members of the investment community. Not forgetting the importance of integrating operational and other nonfinancial information in the comprehensive report, the bottom line also matters significantly. Specifically, the ability of an integrated report to connect to the financial results the operational and nonfinancial initiatives undertaken by an organization makes it appealing and useful. Quantifying and reporting different flows of information from the operational side of the business side, and linking these forces to financial performance represents an important advantage of integrated reporting over previous nonfinancial methodologies. Building a bridge while presenting information and data in a format that is both understandable and relevant, as well as integrating that information into the strategic plan of the entity represent ideas and tactics that appeal to both traditional financial users and nonfinancial stakeholder groups.

Stakeholder theory and the greater influence of stakeholder groups on management decision-making and the analysis of proposed projects and initiatives, appears to be providing a much needed spark in the debate around more comprehensive reporting. Specifically, this debate can assist in generating buy-in and stakeholder support for more comprehensive reporting. That said, in order to translate enthusiasm and interest for a more comprehensive view of financial performance into actual reports and information, the quantitative template adds the most value. Drilling down, one of the fundamental flaws most often associated with nonfinancial or stakeholder reporting is that these different types of information are not usually reported on a consistent basis. Such lack of consistency, in addition to being frustrating for end users of these reports, also limits the effectiveness of this information to the marketplace. Put simply, if end users of nonfinancial information and data cannot rely on, or set benchmarks or expectations associated with these different types of information, the interest and usefulness of these reports will inevitably decrease.

Technology tools, namely the increasing percentage of accounting and financial services work performed by artificial intelligence, analytical platforms, and facilitated via blockchain networks continue to make real-time reporting increasingly possible. Tools and platforms such as these enable accounting professionals, both internal and external to organizations, to make more effective and efficient decisions based on the available data. Increasing the efficiency of decision-making, in addition to improving its effectiveness, is a logical and dual approach to this situation. Resources are not unlimited in nature, thus it is especially important in a globally competitive environment that management professionals and their advisors effectively leverage options as they enter the marketplace.

Even with the greater integration of technology into the business decision-making process, including the IoT, artificial intelligence, and the recent rise and buzz surrounding blockchain technology, data consistency and clarity remains an important issue. Making effective business decisions, inevitably, requires that management teams and the organizations they lead have access to quantitative information, and necessitates constructing an effective qualitative framework. Management professionals are conditioned to expect and use consistent data and information to both plan future decisions, and to evaluate the progress and status of decisions currently underway. To date, sustainability, operational data, and other nonfinancial information have been plagued by inconsistency, a multitude of competing frameworks, and a lack of assurance services to validate or confirm these different types of information. The importance of data management and assurance services may seem like an ancillary topic and area of research, but they are in fact a core component of how integrated reporting will achieve greater adoption. If management professionals are expected to support and utilize an integrated reporting framework, both professional and unprofessional end users must be able to rely on and have faith in the data being produced and reported. Accounting professionals have an important role to play in this process, and this topic will be discussed and analyzed throughout this book.

These inconsistencies in organizational data are both logical and unsurprising considering that every organization is different, has management teams focused on different issues, and has different levels of internal resources available to them to report information. For example, an organization operating in extractive industries such as lumber, oil and natural gas, mining, or power generation would perhaps be most interested in collecting and reporting environmental information. In addition to representing a rather obvious fit, it also provides both internal and external users with important information linked to possible regulatory and legal matters that may arise in the future. While those previous examples make sense, and some other organizations that are arguably higher profile in the marketplace might not be as obvious a fit, they should be as equally interested in sustainability reporting.

Technology and service organizations, particularly in developed and industrialized economies, have come to dominate large swaths and areas of the economic landscape. Sustainability, once viewed as only a concern for organizations in heavy and extractive fields, is increasingly a concern and area of focus for service organizations. For example, companies that conduct the vast majority of their business via the Internet, such as Google, Facebook, Amazon, and Alibaba must maintain large server farms to collect, analyze, and generate insights from the vast amounts of information generated by customers and internal operations. In order to contain, collect, analyze, and report these ever-increasing amounts of data, however, requires that organizations have the necessary information available to them to communicate action-oriented data to stakeholder and shareholder groups. A key differentiator contained in the integrated reporting framework makes this communication possible, and that is the inclusion of a variety of organizationally important data reported in a quantitative framework.

The importance of a comprehensive framework, supported and reinforced by quantitative evidence and information, is difficult to overstate in the context of integrated financial reporting. Coordinating with accounting and financial professionals to create and communicate the information contained within an integrated report is important for several reasons. First, by linking together the strategic goals and initiatives of management—often informed and driven by nonfinancial information and data, with the accounting function will result in more robust analysis and reporting. This increased robustness and clarity on the nonfinancial drivers of organizational performance are also important, as they connect to how the marketplace will react to the implementation of an integrated reporting framework. Obtaining buy-in and support from financial end users of organizational data, including both the financial and nonfinancial information contained within an integrated report, is essential for establishing and sustaining its usefulness.

Last, but not least, is that as accounting and financial professionals become involved in this process, the development of standardized assurance and attestation standards becomes more likely. While the marketplace and associated end users will inevitably expect that reports and information be issued in a consistent and comparable manner, the rigor by which these data are examined is also important. Introduced here, and revisited throughout this book, is the overarching theme that integrated reporting does not simply represent yet another reporting or compliance obligation, or an opportunity to potentially greenwash current organizational activities. Rather, a properly implemented integrated reporting structure enables organizations to quantify, analyze, and report on a wide variety of information and data that drives how the organization performs both in the present and moving forward.

The Business Case for an Integrated Report

Reporting and communicating information to both internal and external stakeholder groups is a duty of management that can, if left unchecked, occupy a substantial majority of management professionals time and attention. Taking into account the increased number of stakeholders who are interested in obtaining a quantitative assessment of the organizations performance, it may seem inefficient to simply add an additional reporting framework to the reporting process. Establishing and reinforcing the business case for an integrated report, however, is not something that can, or should, be taken lightly or approached in a haphazard manner. Building this business case, establishing baseline expectations and requirements for what types of data and information will be contained in this report, and linking integrated reporting to more effective decision-making are critical steps that must be undertaken beginning at the time of implementation. In addition, and in order to obtain and sustain shareholder buy-in and support for this framework, it is imperative that management have an effective analysis and understanding of just how integrated reporting facilitates more effective decision-making. To offset the usual complications and pushback associated with increasing reporting requirements, illustrating the business potential and ability of integrated reporting to increase the effectiveness of organizational decision-making is a key step in increasing the adoption of an integrated reporting framework.

Specifically, drilling down into the proverbial nuts and bolts of an integrated report, there are several factors and identifying pieces of information that can, and should, be used to help illustrate and highlight how integrated reporting can help facilitate business decision-making. Integrating the operational details and information related to core business functions into the decision-making process that already exists in the organization is a logical place to begin the implementation and analysis of integrated reporting into an increasing number of industries. For example, for an organization that operates within the logistical and shipping industry it would make sense to take into account the importance of manufactured capital, as well as the increasing importance of social and relational capital in the marketplace. Analyzing an organization such as Amazon, which increasingly operates in the logistical arena with a web portal to facilitate purchases and other interactions, the growing impact of manufactured capital and associated investments is difficult to overstate. Connecting the business operations and value proposition of the organization to the integrated reporting framework is imperative for making its adoption and implementation a continued success.

Linking the reporting framework to both business operations and information communicated to both internal and external stakeholders also requires that management professionals assess and be aware of the information contained both in the organization and current reporting framework. Preparing this coordinated assessment allows both financial and nonfinancial stakeholders to participate in and drive the decision-making process within the organization. Last, but perhaps most importantly, is the integration of information and data from a variety of internal sources to external deliverables. Making sure the wide array of information produced and managed by organizations is effectively communicated can make the difference between the success or failure of different initiatives.

An analysis and justification of an integrated reporting framework would be incomplete if the following reality was not acknowledged—management professionals need to be able to build and sustain value in the short, medium, and long term. Specifically, and this is something well known to internal management but which can sometimes be overlooked by external analysts is that operational data are what drives the financial results and performance of the organization. Harnessing the reams of information and data produced internally by the organization, quantifying these streams of information, and reporting these different types of data are important first steps to maximizing the value of operational data. Competing and sustaining a competitive advantage in a globalized and digitized business landscape requires agility, adaptability, and the willingness to leverage all available information. Integrated reporting, while not a cure-all for the gaps in current reporting, provides a template that allow organizations and external analysts to better understand just what is driving the firm moving forward.

Put simply, and based on the available market information connected to both the integrated reporting framework and the increased diversity of stakeholder received organizational information, it does appear that there is a business case for the development and implementation of such a framework. Taking into account the fact that the broader business environment is influenced by a variety of different information streams and types of information, the business case for reporting this information in a consistent manner is difficult to overstate. Making effective decisions, from a managerial perspective and point of view, requires that the management team has access to, and be able to make effective use of, these different sources of information. As such, this appears to be a logical place to begin the examination as to what exact type of information and data are contained in the integrated reporting framework. Answering this question may seem logical, but it is an important part of how integrated reported is adapted over time by different organizations.

What Information Is in an Integrated Report?

Underlying the reporting framework of integrated reporting is the reality that both internal and external decision makers require a wide variety of information in order to effectively evaluate the performance of the organization. Across the business landscape, and including a variety of different industry lines and entities, management professionals are increasingly expected to make decisions with both a shareholder and stakeholder perspective in mind. An ongoing issue, despite the increased interest and importance in these varieties of information, has been the lack of consistency and comparability contained in nonfinancial reports and dashboards. Integrated reporting and information contained within this reporting framework must deliver additional value to both internal and external users in order to facilitate increased adoption. Included within this framework, from a positive perspective, is the reality that in order to deliver information relevant to decision makers it must initially be presented in a familiar and comparable framework.

Included in the framework and model of reporting, which is embedded in integrated reporting, is the idea of a multiple capital model. Such an idea and framework, representing the quantification and comparability of a variety of information, provides management and external users of organizational information with several benefits. First, from an internal management perspective, the requirements and resources necessary to quantify and report information necessitate changes in both internal controls and processes to generate this information on an ongoing basis. While management professionals and stakeholders are clearly increasingly interested in broader ranges of information, there can often be a lack of communication and processes in place to deliver this information. Tweaking and changing the internal processes and controls required to generate these different types of information will inevitably involve increased investments in both personnel and resources. More on this topic will be discussed further in this book, but this is an important fact to keep in mind when integrated reporting is discussed and analyzed in the context of a broader business situation.

Second, communication with both stakeholders and shareholders is both a prerogative of management and increasingly a requirement in an interconnected business landscape, which is nearly overwhelmed by information and expecting management to deliver effective results and information. Specifically, and included in the framework and mindset of integrated reporting is the idea of a multiple capital model, that is, different types of information and capital generate positive or negative results for the organization. This reality and acknowledgment, while not appearing to be any sort of ground breaking or innovative change, does appear to reinforce the shift of management to a stakeholder-oriented model of business management and practice. A differentiating factor contained in the integrated reporting framework, however, is the concept of a multiple capital model. While at first glance the inclusion of yet another framework or model might not seem to be terribly important or different, nor a true way to add value to the reporting process, this only represents an incomplete view. Examining further this idea of a multiple capital model reveals that this inclusion and addition to the integrated reporting framework address the gap in communication that is consistently an issue with regards to communicating and disseminating nonfinancial data.

Prior to diving into a more comprehensive analysis of what specific types of data are contained within different types of capital included within this model, it is worth noting just how important a consistent delivery method is for further implementation. Management professionals, both those employed by the organization and those taking a look at organizational data from an external perspective, require and expect quantitative information. Arguably even more important, however, is that the information is delivered and reported on a continuous basis and can be compared to prior periods, while containing meaningful information for decision makers. Financial information is already reported on a periodic basis to end users, and there is a long standing framework that can be used to compare and analyze these classes of information. In spite of whatever flaws may exist in the current reporting methodologies, all involved parties are aware of what information is included and what these data represent.

Increasingly, operational information is also overtly reported to internal management professionals on an ongoing basis, which is important for strategic planning and execution decisions. As more and more data are collected, analyzed, and reported via a variety of different platforms and as the IoT ecosystem grows, the importance and usefulness of quantifying and standardizing these data will grow. Circling back, one of the key flaws and shortcomings of prior sustainability metrics and reporting methods is that the information is presented in a consistent quantitative manner. The multiple capital model provides an important bridge between the massive amounts of information available to internal and external users, and the ability for this information to be used to make better business decisions. Building on this concept further and examining the different types of capital is a logical next step in this process.

The Multiple Capital Model

Capital, in a traditional business sense, represents the financial resources available to the management of an organization to help make effective business decisions; however, this definition does not appear to be satisfactory in the current business context. Instead, and reflecting the broader reality that organizations must operate in, a more comprehensive definition of capital appears to be appropriate. One such definition and a more comprehensive example of capital would read something like the following—capital represents the totality of information and resources available to management to achieve the business objectives of the organization. New definitions, in and of themselves, will not be able to enact a change in the business reporting landscape, nor lead to the necessary change a quantitative framework including different types of capital will require.

This redefinition of capital, in terms of what it means for specific organizations and the overall business landscape, may seem like a minor change at first glance but in fact it represents a fundamental shift in how organizations may operate and move forward. Capital clearly has a strong financial connotation, and this is perfectly logical as it connects to the fiduciary duty of every management team. Regardless of industry, the core fiduciary duty of management professionals is to create value for the organization, and a benchmark by which this can be evaluated is whether or not the organization creates more value and assets than are consumed during operations. While this is a baseline, however, it is all too often the only metric and piece of information used to judge the worthiness of an organizational plan and associated management team. As has been illustrated time and again, either through organizational failure, fraud, or unethical activity, simply evaluating an organization purely on financial terms is insufficient for analysts seeking to obtain a comprehensive view of how the organization is performing. Especially in a stakeholder environment (where stakeholders increasingly exercise influence and voice opinions on organizational direction), redefining and expanding the definition of capital is essential.

The multiple capital model, illustrated in Figure 2.1 lies at the core of the integrated reporting framework, and differentiates this reporting construct from other options currently in the marketplace. Linking back to the earlier conversation and content regarding the quantification of operational information, the ultimate goal of this quantification must be that this information is now assembled in a context and format usable for management professionals. Integrated reporting, not perfect by any definition, does provide a framework for management teams to analyze, quantify, and report these various streams of data that already exist inside the firm. This may seem like a simple idea and construct, but it represents a fundamental shift in how information is communicated both internally and externally for market use.

Taken in the context of how organizations must operate and engage with a stakeholder-oriented landscape, simply viewing capital as a strictly financial item will only provide a partial view of the impact capital has on the decision-making process. Integrated reporting, while clearly and concisely reporting the financial position and performance of the organization, also attempts to communicate how these results are produced. Capital, viewed in the context of stakeholder decision-making, can and

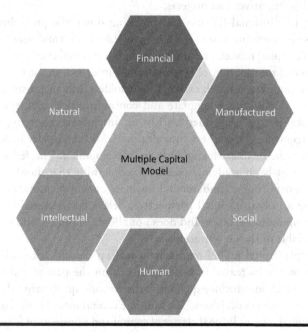

Figure 2.1   The multiple capital model.

does take the form of both financial and operational information. Operational data and the specific streams of information and data that matter most will, of course, be different among various organizations, but every company and management team must be able to understand and quantify the connection between operations and financial results. This may seem like a simplistic concept, but in reality the disconnect between operations and financial management of an organization can be stark, even in this age of increased analytics and the IoT.

Simply producing vast reams of operational information does not appear to be a logical process to facilitate more comprehensive reporting and analysis. In order to effectively leverage the increased amounts of information available to the management teams across industry lines, there must be a framework and construct in place to consistently and comparably report this information. Connecting these concepts, the production and availability of information and the integration of greater types of information is where the true value added by the multiple capital model comes into play. Specifically, building this model and recognizing the fact that doing so will take time will enable more comprehensive reporting and analysis by management professionals for two distinct reasons. First, the obligation and expectation that reporting will include both financial and nonfinancial information will drive changes on an internal basis. Drilling down in order to actually produce this more comprehensive type of reporting and information, internal functional groups and divisions must be able to communicate in a cost-efficient and effective manner, that is, reducing some of the internal friction and obstacles that all too often hamstring initiatives and projects.

Reducing this internal friction and breaking down the proverbial silos that divide employees represents one of the most tangible upsides and benefits associated with a multiple capital model. Friction, whether it is internal friction that delays the production and dissemination of organizational information, or external friction that makes communication with external stakeholders difficult, costs organizations time and money. Building a template and communication tool, specifically the multiple capital model embedded within an integrated reporting framework, enables management to spend less time dealing with shareholder issues and more time managing the business for growth and development. The reduction of this friction is not merely an academic exercise or something that should be viewed as an ancillary benefit, but a fundamental business benefit of integrated reporting. Friction, from an organizational perspective, delays decision-making, consumes resources in unproductive tasks, and does not allow the organization to maximize resources available to the organization.

The multiple capital model represents a realization and acknowledgement of the fact that despite increased interest and focus on the part of stakeholders and management, which may include qualitative discussions, quantitative data drives the vast majority of business decisions. The multiple capital model includes in addition to financial capital, five additional classes of capital and information for management professional to reference and review. These additional types of capital include natural,

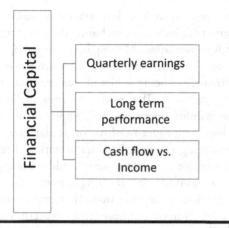

Figure 2.2   Connecting natural capital to financial performance.

social and relational, manufactured, intellectual, and human capitals. Built directly into the multiple capital model—and the integrated reporting structure itself, is the underlying importance and emphasis of a broader array of information and data for management professionals to use and report to external users. Reiterating a prior issue often associated with nonfinancial reporting and information, quantifying these different types of data and information is a challenge, but examples of these different capitals can help illustrate the applicability of these ideas to organizations.

Financial capital is perhaps the most commonly analyzed, reported, and discussed class of capital either consumed or produced by an organization; therefore, it is a logical place to begin this comparison and analysis. While not representing an inherently new terminology or idea, when placed alongside the other capitals embedded within the multiple capital model, the contrasts and differences become readily apparent (Figure 2.2).

Natural Capital

The concept of natural capital might appear to be the simplest to understand and the most directly linked to the current business environment, and that is a logical perspective due to the increased pressure on organizations to operate in an environmentally sustainable manner. Sustainability reporting is already underway in an overwhelming percentage of publicly traded organizations in the United States. Interestingly, particularly with regards to sustainability and other environmentally oriented reporting, the United States has traditionally lagged other markets in this area. Such adoption, when viewed in this context, is even more significant and indicative of the increasing importance of environmental and sustainability data to business decision-making. Focusing specifically on examples of natural capital appears to be a logical place to begin the conversation and analysis related to implementation.

Sustainability is a trending topic in the marketplace, and one that has an effect on organizations in a variety of industries, including those that may not initially appear to be involved in this conversation. Making better use of operational information, especially information connected to how the organization is performing and how the financial performance is being achieved, represents a fact that should be of interest to every organization. That said, and even in light of increased focus and interest in sustainability operations, it is important for internal and external users to be on the lookout for greenwashing or similar short-term tactics. Putting together and implementing a standardized framework and reporting structure for communicating information and data appears to address many of the shortcomings and gaps in the current nonfinancial reporting options utilized in the marketplace.

As mentioned previously, organizations that operate in extractive or other environmentally intensive lines of business will focus on the impact these operations have on the broader business environment. An example of an organization that has successfully integrated these types of information is Coca-Cola, focusing on water sustainability, sustainable operations, and recycling water used in continuing operations. Labeled the water stewardship report, the quantification and consistent reporting of environmental data provides several benefits to internal and external users. First, from an internal management point of view, the importance of water to the core business of Coca-Cola—beverages—is abundantly clear, but such reporting quantifies just how important it is. What is measured, whether it is in the form of metrics and other reporting tools, is inevitably the information and data that forms the basis for the strategic decision-making process.

Second, and perhaps even more importantly in the context of natural capital and achieving a more comprehensive report, are the financial benefits and information generated by quantifying these types of sustainability information. Every resource does clearly have a cost, but often times the actual costs cannot be captured using traditional financial models, and connecting financial and operational data, may not be consistently reported over time. Leveraging advances in technology to more effectively quantify and analyze these different streams of information is an important differentiating factor contained within the integrated reporting framework. Natural capital can be perhaps most effectively summarized as the financial impact of sustainability efforts on the organization, such as the information communicated by Coca-Cola to the marketplace. We will return to the analysis of Coca-Cola in more depth later in this book, but it is certainly worth introducing the organization and topic here to initiate the conversation around natural capital (Figure 2.3).

Value Add of Natural Capital

Any reporting framework or idea has to, in addition to providing information to the marketplace, be connected to the value an organization produces and delivers to stakeholder groups. The topics of sustainability and the reporting of sustainability and other environmental types of information, however, has not traditionally been

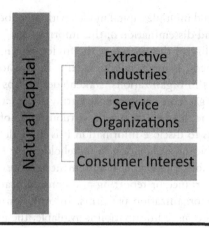

Figure 2.3   Applications for natural capital.

viewed within the context of delivering value. Rather, these classes and types of information have often been associated with compliance of other regulatory pressure; however, this represents an incomplete view of just how important environmental data can be for ongoing operations. Specifics vary from organization to organization and from industry to industry, but several fundamentals remain consistent across industry and geographic lines.

For example, capital intensive industries and organization, such as those that operate in extractive industries and businesses, have a clear motivation to report and quantify this information—and many already are. Taking a step back, however, and viewing this situation from the perspective of longer-term value creation and organizational success, it becomes apparent that reporting these types of data can also lead to substantial financial benefits. Getting out in front of possible operational issues and taking advantage of digitization to track operations in real time allows management to be proactive instead of reactive, as pertaining to reporting and other informational issues. Simply being aware of potential issues, including looming environmental regulations and other industry specific changes is not sufficient—management must be able to look forward and use this information to make effective business decisions.

Namely, by taking advantage of the increased monitoring and focus-integrated reporting, and the multiple capital model requires of organizations, it enables the management teams to actually leverage this information instead of just reporting it. By default, via the creation of a natural capital account and classification requires that organizations and their associated management personnel pay closer attention to how these different flows of information affect the organization. Specifically, the financial impact and implications of environmental and operational issues are not minor or insignificant in nature, and can have a dramatic impact on the current and projected financial performance of an organization moving forward. Paying increased attention, however, is just one upside and benefit of adopting an integrated reporting framework and multiple capital model, with other benefits associated with the communication and dissemination of this information.

Analyzing the reality of the situation, the underlying market truth of "what is measured is managed" is increasingly evident. If, due to actions undertaken by management teams in organizations, stakeholder groups are familiarized and accustomed to receiving a more comprehensive array of data, their expectations will not fade away over time. Rather, creating a virtuous cycle of reinforcement, once an organization begins to disclose information it is difficult to stop or adjust this course without a significant explanation to stakeholders. At first glance this might appear to be simply another reporting requirement and obstacle, but it reinforces and solidifies the importance or reporting and communicating data inextricably connected to how the organization performs. Information is how organizations make decisions, and the more information is available, the greater the probability of effective decisions.

Social and Relational Capital

Social and relational capital may seem like a term and idea better situated in a human resources conversation, or a dialogue better suited to a management conversation, but it only represents a partial view of this capital area. Two distinct areas and implications linked to this type of capital appear to be most appropriate— the connection between an organization and its customers and between the organization with the credit markets. Taken in the context of a business landscape where management professionals are answerable to both financial and nonfinancial stakeholders both areas appear important for decision-making. Obtaining the appropriate levels of information linked to these areas can be challenging, especially for the social category linking customer analytics to capital creation. Just because it is challenging, however, does not mean that this task is either impossible nor worth management time—to the contrary it is worth both.

Connections between customers and management teams are currently an important aspect of management responsibility, and only appears to be increasing as the business landscape becomes more digitized and connected. Examples of both positive and negative feedbacks driven by customers abound among publicly traded firms, with the subsequent effects creating or destroying billions in stock market value very quickly. Arguably more important than any short to medium impact on the valuation of the company, however, is the viral nature of customer opinion. As much as social media and digitization allows for increased organizational efficiency and agility, it also provides customers and other stakeholder groups with a global real-time platform to express opinions and document experiences. Managing these interactions and the expectations of customers, as expressed via social media, is a reasonable next step on the path to quantifying this information. Documenting these results and reporting these sets of information to senior management can also provide management with the information necessary to successfully engage with various stakeholder groups.

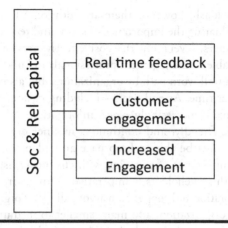

Figure 2.4 Components of social and relational capital.

Raising capital, whether it is from investors interested in contributing capital, or creditors interested in providing medium to long-term financing to organizations, is an activity that provides liquidity to firms large and small. Obtaining sufficient capital and engaging in a continuous dialogue with shareholders and creditors is critical, especially for management teams seeking to foster a transition from short-term to a longer-term growth arc. Communication is often overlooked as an important part of pivoting from a quarterly earnings model to one that emphasizes a more comprehensive view of growth. Relational capital and the ability of management professionals to have continuous and effective dialogue with providers of financial capital can be pivoted in several ways. Quantifying the number and type of interactions between the management team and external capital providers seems an appropriate place to initiate an analysis of the possible use cases for social and relational capital. Following this initial analysis, and dependent on what information is gleaned from it additional steps can and should be taken (Figure 2.4).

Use Case

The use cases and information from social and relational capital are self-evident from even a cursory review of the media and business landscape. Social media, whether it is delivered via platforms such as Facebook, Twitter, Instagram, or video platforms such as YouTube is increasingly the way consumers and other stakeholder groups receive information and data. This may seem like a trend and story only applicable to certain organizations that operate in the media, news, or entertainment industries but it is a powerful trend driving management decision-making across industry lines. Creating and maintaining robust and healthy relationships with different stakeholder groups, including customers, is increasingly a role and duty of management, which can make or break certain projects or initiatives. Besides the social media backlash, however, there are additional factors that should be considered when evaluating the importance of social and relational capital.

Engaging customers, leveraging the cost effectiveness of social media, and using the tools available to management professionals to build brand ambassadors is both a tactic and a well-worn path by organizations, but also a methodology and concept evolving over time. As end users—including customers and stakeholders at an institutional level—increasingly expect information and data to be delivered in a concise, mobile friendly, and continuous manner organizations and their management teams must be able to keep pace and adapt to these expectations. In addition to the importance of engaging with customers, establishing networks and connections with stakeholders is imperative in an environment increasingly dependent on collaboration and cooperation among different organizations. Virtually every multinational organization, and many smaller to medium-sized enterprises, are a component in a supply chain linked to other organizations. Maintaining good relations with these organizations is of course important for continued business success, but there is an additional component of relational capital that may not be as readily apparent.

Coordinating the flow of information, from a supply chain and logistical perspective, can increasingly be elevated to the same position as financial investments or strategic decision-making in other areas. Delivering information, goods, and services to a variety of end users, which include both customers and other partner organizations, is a core competency that can, and often does, differentiate firms in the marketplace. Working with other organizations in the supply chain and network of the organization in question allows management to not only generate insights related to their business, but also to create action-oriented plans to facilitate the communication of information and value between different network members. Looking further and connecting the idea of integrated reporting to other changes, specifically technological changes such as blockchain technology and platforms, seems to present a viable business opportunity. Blockchain and the associated implications of this technology can in essence be thought of as the underlying platform that other applications can operate and run on, such as Bitcoin and other cryptocurrencies. That said, it is important to expand the scope and analysis linked to blockchain technology and the blockchain platform to account for the changes positioned to impact both how supply chains operate, and how these changes to supply chain information drive changes in stakeholder relationships.

Manufactured Capital

The concept and idea of manufactured capital is relatively straightforward to understand and analyze at a conceptual level, but it applies to larger percentage of organizations than might initially be apparent. Manufactured capital does not apply exclusively to long-term assets or plant, property, and equipment but rather is a representation of the importance of infrastructure in a digitized business landscape.

While consumers and other ultimate end users may transact and engage in purchases in a virtual or online environment, the fulfillment of online business and digital transactions requires physical infrastructure. Organizations focused in the logistics business and fulfillment processes will clearly focus the largest amount of time and energy on quantifying manufactured capital, but the concept of manufactured capital is applicable to virtually all organizations. Acknowledging this reality—that manufactured capital can apply to both plant property and equipment—opens the dialogue about this tool and its applicability to a broader set of organizations.

Beginning with the an analysis of an organization such as Alibaba, Amazon, FedEx, DHL, or UPS the implications and connections between manufactured capital and sustainable success are evident. In short, if the organization is unable to create and maintain sufficient levels of manufactured capital and assets the management team will be unable to deliver results stakeholders and shareholders expect. Specific ratios and metrics that can and should be used to evaluate the effectiveness of manufactured capital in the broader context of business decisions may include, but are not limited to, the following. Net investment in plant, property, and equipment, including the reporting of trends related to these investments are of importance from a purely financial perspective and a more comprehensive perspective. Plant, property, and equipment, from a financial and traditional reporting point of view, has an impact on the balance sheet, income statement, and statement of cash flows. Often overlooked in the analysis of sales, income, and earnings growth, depreciation and the investment decisions made by management professionals are the impact these decsiions have on short, medium, and long term results. Specifically, it is important to note that not every decision will have an equivalent impact when framed in the context of different time horizons.

Taking a more detailed look, it is clear that a financial analysis of the plant, property, and equipment decisions made by the management team at the organization also will drive how the organization performs over time. From a stakeholder perspective, management should be making investment decisions and choices with both financial shareholders and stakeholders in mind, and manufactured capital is an effective representation of this perspective. Organizations must make investments and choices during both cycles of economic growth and periods of economic recession, to enable the organization to succeed in moving forward. Manufactured capital, and the investments made to either create or improve assets linked to this capital category, are linked to the improvement of communication and information dissemination critical to the implementation of a multiple capital model and integrated report. Specifically, making certain investment choices and allocating resources toward improving the infrastructure of the business might result in lower than expected short-term results. Management teams must have the internal support, usually at the Board of Directors' level, and the information at hand to effectively advocate for these types of decisions. An interesting development and inclusion with the integrated reporting framework is that intellectual capital

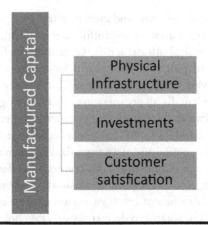

Figure 2.5 Connecting manufactured capital from investments to customer satisfaction.

is also included in the conversation and dialogue as related to broader business objectives and goals (Figure 2.5).

Use Case

Manufactured capital viewed at the most simplistic and high level perspective is an idea and concept that relates to both physical assets created and utilized by an organization, as well as the manufactured capital created through research and development initiatives. Beginning with the use case associated with physical assets, such as plant, property, and equipment leveraged in business operations, the connection is clear. Prior to drilling down, however, it is important to acknowledge the two following points that are important for organizations doing business both in the United States and in overseas markets. First, there is a distinct and significant difference between how physical assets are accounted for under generally accepted accounting principles (GAAP), and accounting methodologies required for tax reporting purposes. These differences, both in the initial cost recorded on the balance sheets and how manufactured assets, including physical assets, are accounted for on a continuous basis, can distort financial performance in the medium and long-term.

While depreciation is a noncash expense and is not directly linked or related to the ongoing operations of the business, decisions made by management whether or not to invest in these physical assets are critical for organizational growth. Metrics that are appear especially applicable for this situation include the ratio of investment dollars in the current year versus depreciation expenses. Investing dollars in the continuing development of physical and manufactured assets will inevitably absorb cash flows and other resources in the current period; these investments lay the foundation and groundwork for future business opportunities in the medium and long term. While the connection between the development and investment of physical assets represents a clear connection between manufactured capital and current accounting reporting requirements, the linkage between this concept and intangible assets may appear to be less clear in the current environment.

Intangible assets, although not physical in nature nor possessing any of the physical characteristics of what is normally considered to be a manufactured asset, contain many of the same benefits and costs associated with physical assets. Intangible assets, like brand equity, copyrights, and trademark development require a longer-term perspective to be utilized by the organization, and will also require investments of both financial and personnel resources. Additionally, they will also require changes to both internal and external systems that facilitate traditional reporting requirements, but which appear insufficient in the current stakeholder environment. Building and acknowledging the value embedded in intangible assets is a challenge currently facing the accounting and finance landscape, but it is one that the profession, via developments and advances in the accounting profession, will be able to meet. Especially since the total value of intangible and intellectual assets are estimated in the trillions of dollars, this is not an area that should be ignored or viewed as immaterial. Linking back to the integrated reporting concept, the development of a more robust reporting and communication template for intellectual assets is a market imperative.

Intellectual Capital

Intellectual capital—closely linked but not equivalent to intellectual property—is an important type of capital and information which only appears to be increasing in importance as it pertains to creating and sustaining a competitive advantage in the medium to long term. Intellectual property, not a new or unheard of term or idea, is linked very closely to intangible assets and other types of items, including but not limited to copyrights, patents, and other types of service-related assets. Much has been written about intellectual property, and that will not be reiterated here, but we will rather attempt to focus on the linkage between intellectual property, intellectual assets, and the connection between these topics and integrated financial reporting.

One specific difference between intellectual property and intellectual capital is that the latter takes into account the necessary tools and organizational infrastructure to not only develop these assets, but also to safeguard and protect them in an environment beset by data hacks and breaches. A business environment routinely featuring hacks and breaches of organizations large and small across industry lines clearly illustrates the importance of these informations and assets for the success of an organization. Taken within this more comprehensive perspective, intellectual capital builds upon the ideas and concepts of intellectual property while also incorporating strategies and tactics to maximize the impact of these assets to create organizational value.

Some of the specific ideas and methods by which intellectual capital can be quantified and reported include, but are not limited to the following: (1) does the

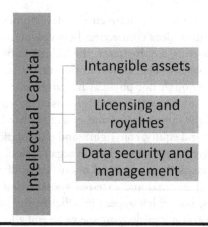

Figure 2.6 Examples of intellectual capital.

organization have a comprehensive policy related to tracking, organizing, and evaluating the current status of intellectual assets? The first step in maximizing the value of these assets, logically enough, requires the management team to be equipped to accurately and comprehensively analyze various intellectually linked assets; (2) are the different classes of intellectual assets and capital, including but not limited to items like patents and trademarks, leveraged effectively to generate positive financial performance for the organization? Specifically, are appropriate joint venture, licensing, and product development plans and opportunities leveraged comprehensively? Making use of various intellectual assets and capital can provide management professionals with a competitive edge that is both difficult to replicate and costly for competitors to reverse engineer (Figure 2.6); and (3) an important item to mention in any conversation linked to intellectual capital or assets is the cyber security policy in place around intellectual assets and capital, and whether or not management is investing sufficient resources in these efforts. Simply spending increased funds on these measures is insufficient, however, and financial resources invested in tools must be coordinated with education, training, and continuous learning around these items as well. Intellectual capital, building on the platform and foundation of intellectual property, necessitates that management professionals take stock of both current efforts and planning for future efforts in these areas. Making investments, leveraging existing assets to maximize performance, and taking a holistic approach toward service and intellectually related assets make sense in the short, medium, and long term.

Use Case

With the value of organizations increasingly allocated to the intellectual and intangible assets of organizations, the importance of reporting and analyzing these assets and related investments is increasingly important for management professionals. In addition to some of the suggestions and guidelines outlined above regarding intellectual capital, which are important for valuation purposes, better utilization and reporting of intellectual and intangible assets can also help orient management time and energy. It will clearly continue to be important to develop and invest in physical assets but with virtually every asset increasingly affected and digitized in nature, or at least augmented by technology, focusing on intangible and intellectual capital is not a topic that should be ignored. This does represent a challenge, especially under current accounting standards that do not allow recognition of internally generated intangible assets, but this does not mean management is without tools or tactics.

Connecting to the idea of integrated financial reporting, which represents an inclusive and more comprehensive analysis of organizational performance, intellectual and intangible assets have an important role to play in this discussion. Accounting for and quantifying the current effects and impact of these data flows are, obviously, an important task for management, but these flows of information can also be used in the following two areas: the value and utilization of assets can augment and improve the business, and create business opportunities. Industrial organizations, including industry giants such as General Electric and Siemens, are continuing to invest billons of financial resources into augmenting and improving current industrial product and service offerings. This connection between intellectual assets and investments in technological assets to ongoing business operations is a direct value-add management teams can reference in explaining investment choices to stakeholder groups.

Bridging the gap, and juggling the expectations of financial stakeholders versus those of other shareholder groups is a tactic and connection that dovetails directly with integrated reporting and current reporting standards. While it is increasingly evident that organizations must invest both financial and personnel resources, justifying the often large amounts of capital expenditures necessary to achieve an industrial scale can be difficult to justify in any sort of challenging financial environment. Even in the best of times, investing large amounts of financial resources into projects oriented toward the future can be difficult and requires funneling profits from currently profitable operations to fund uncertain initiatives. Explaining the rationale and connecting the investments made now to the strategic plan and projects underway in the organization can provide both background to investors and additional information to stakeholder groups. Especially in a stakeholder-oriented landscape, that is increasingly globalized in nature, making sufficient and ongoing investments in organizational assets is critical for success in the medium and long term. Making these investments and connecting them to intangible assets and technology tools is simply the first step of this process. Second, and arguably most important for connecting improved financial performance to integrated reporting, is that quantifying operational results connects these results of the organization directly to the financial results. While such a connection may seem obvious to internal management professionals, communicating the importance of investing for longer-term growth to market analysts does represent a shift in the market conversation. Especially as data becomes increasingly valuable over time and across industry lines, protecting, investing in, and effectively managing information will continue to increase in importance over time.

Human Capital

The idea of human capital, when initially introduced and discussed, may seem not applicable to financial management or financial reporting. Instead, the idea of managing employees, maximizing their efficiency, and leveraging existing competencies is usually a task delegated to human resource professionals or the personnel department. Such a perspective, however, only presents a partial and incomplete view of both the topic of human capital and the importance of human capital for organizational success. Employees, despite the numerous advances in technology tools—including but not limited to blockchain and artificial intelligence—represent the true drivers of innovation and growth in an organization. Even in an era of rapid technological advancement in the form of scalable tools such as IBM Watson (already being implemented at a number of service organizations), investing and managing employees effectively is imperative.

Quantifying the value and worth of employees from a financial reporting perspective has traditionally been to simply include employees as one of the costs of doing business on the income statement. Framed in the context of a more comprehensive view of organizational performance and management, categorizing employees as expense items is neither accurate nor reflective of the value they deliver. Even more important for management is that merely tracking spending on employee initiatives is not sufficient when attempting to quantify some of the information and data linked to human capital. Funding different projects and initiatives from a purely financial perspective does not encompass the reality of just how important human capital is to sustained success. Depending on the study referenced, between half and two-thirds of employees reportedly are disengage in the workplace, which inevitably has a dramatic financial impact on organizations across industry lines In the context of this research, effectively managing employees and embedded competencies is critical. In a business landscape driven by intellectual capital and intangible assets across industry and geography lines, achieving continued and proactive employee engagement is a core responsibility of management teams.

Looking at specifically just how human capital can be quantified, it is worthwhile to consider this idea from a holistic perspective. The areas concerned include, but are not limited to, the amount of time spent on training and development, turnover ratios in the organization, leadership depth and engagement with employees, and employee engagement. Spending and offering different programs in the organization is a logical first step for management professionals to take when seeking to develop and quantify human capital. Investing in employee training and development should be viewed as similar to making investments in different kinds of assets. Especially in a business environment and landscape being rapidly impacted by a number of dramatic changes, continuously developing employee skills at all levels is not an optional activity. While it is important for specific trainings and educational offerings to be tailored to relevant topics for a specific organizationensuring that employees are up to date on current trends and technologies is always advisable.

Employee training and development is directly tied to the success a firm will have in retaining employees. Regardless of geographic location, industry affiliation, or years of experience in the workforce an underlying trend and desire among employees is to have opportunities for development and growth. Retaining employees, especially in a competitive business landscape, is an important differentiator between organizations that generate success in a sustainable manner and those that do not. With the average cost of hiring, training, and onboarding new employees averaging approximately 200%–300% more than existing employee salaries, this is not an issue that can be delegated exclusively to human resources. Management professionals across the organization must be aware of both the positive impact of training and retaining employees, as well as the negative consequences of not doing so in a consistent manner.

Leadership in an organization is labeled a number of different things, including corporate governance and the tone at the top within a company. Regardless of the specific label or title assigned to the concept of leadership depth and management culture, the importance of management attitude and culture plays a large role on organizational success. Numerous examples litter the business landscape with organizations that have failed due to failings of corporate culture and governance. Volkswagen and Wells Fargo might have attracted the most headlines and financial penalties for unethical and fraudulent behavior, but companies such as Uber, Google, and even Facebook have also generated negative consequences for management professionals and their organizations.

Employee engagement surveys and other feedback tools may be initially viewed as a lukewarm solution to the question of how to quantify human capital, but they do serve an important purpose. Measuring and ranking employee feedback and opinion over time, and constructing a culture (linking back to the importance of leadership) provides management with several insights. First, it allows management to see what employee concerns and interests are at any particularly moment in time, which assists with retention efforts, engagement initiatives, and the capability of management to engage in continuous dialogue. Second, it reinforces the positive messages being sent from senior leadership, that is, feedback and actions taken as a result of these surveys can help boost employee morale. Last, and perhaps most important from a human capital perspective, this approach and information provides management with a concrete plan to approach and address the variety of issues linked to employee development and retention (Figure 2.7).

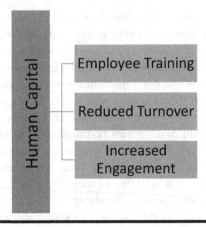

Figure 2.7   How human capital can be put into practice.

Use Case

The use case and business applications for the greater integration and implementation of a human capital model is not something that can usually be pinned down or associated with one specific financial metric. Furthermore, it is increasingly important in a technology driven business environment and landscape that the training, development, and education of employees is viewed as imperative for organizations to succeed. Regardless of the specific platform referenced or implemented by a specific company, or via industry-wide adoption, the underlying change and shift toward more technological integration is clear. It is rather evident to management personnel interested in such matters that investing in training and employee education programs may result in long-term benefits, higher retention, and improved morale. In a financial landscape dominated by short-term results it can be difficult to continue making these investments in both good times and bad.

Commonly, when economic factors result in a downturn or even a recession, organizations tend to lay off employees. Contrasting this—creating a whipsaw effect both internally and in the labor market—is the hiring that almost always occurs during an economic uptick or increase in economic activity. Smoothing out these ups and downs may be difficult and perhaps impossible in some circumstances, but utilizing an integrated reporting framework appears to offer a way to assist this effort. Making investments in employee development and training generate long-term benefits and this is the connection that should be emphasized in the reporting process. Circling back to the integrated reporting framework, it is important for management to remember the underlying purpose of this reporting structure. In an effort to offset some of the short-termism that continues to dominate management decision-making, an integrated reporting framework emphasizes not only different sources and types of capital but also a longer-term vision of how the organization should report and communicate information.

Human capital, building off of a quantitative foundation of cost savings and efficiencies possible due to lower turnover and increased retention, can be expanded and connected directly to the financial benefits and metrics already identifitablet. While it is readily apparent—and reinforced by numerous quantitative studies—that reducing turnover and increasing retention improves financial results in the short term, management professionals have an opportunity—and arguably a responsibility, to connect short-term results to long-term strategy. Investing in employees, developing robust development and education programs, and creating a culture of learning are no longer simply nice things to do. In a digitally connected and technology driven business environment, they may form the basis of sustainable competitive advantages for moving forward.

Differentiating Integrated Reporting

With all of the different frameworks and options in the marketplace, and even with the inclusion of the multiple capital within the reporting structure, an underlying question is how to differentiate integrated reporting in a crowded marketplace. One fundamental difference is that such a framework includes both financial and nonfinancial information in a comprehensive report. Other reporting initiatives and ideas, including sustainability reporting and other types of nonfinancial information, do not include equivalent financial data and metrics. Integrated reporting by its very nature and construct contains both financial and nonfinancial information, which is reported in a quantitative and consistent manner. Echoing back to the very nature of an integrated report, the inclusion of a variety of information in a comparable and consistent framework addresses some of the flaws in nonfinancial reporting.

Differentiating integrated reporting from other reporting frameworks and options is critically important if management proponents are interested in achieving increased adoption and consistent implementation across industry lines. Merely categorizing or emphasizing integrated reporting as yet another reporting construct or obligation is not a recommended path forward for adoption and utilization. Building on the underlying purpose of the reporting framework itself, the emphasis and focus on longer-term finance and strategic planning provides a more logical use case to illustrate in conversations and debates. Shareholders and stakeholder groups alike are well aware of the importance of investing capital for medium and long-term growth, but they have often lacked a framework or methodology with which to communicate efforts in this area. Implementing integrated reporting will inevitably take time to do so appropriately, but constructing the business case associated with this framework assists in this conversation and dialogue.

For example, after analyzing one of the many examples of integrated reporting available through several resources, there are several factors and components worthy of additional analysis. First, by integrating different classes of information, and doing so in a framework such as the multiple capital model, nonfinancial information is quantified and reported in a familiar manner. This apparently slight detail and change from alternative financial templates and options is of critical importance for increased adoption and implementation, since data are what ultimately drives the decision-making process. Reporting information in such a manner allows management professionals to compare and disseminate these operationally important types of data and information. Since operational data and results are what ultimately drive the financial performance of the organization, having these types of information and data presented in a consistent format adds significant value to the reporting process. Emphasizing the importance of this connection, between operational information and the financial performance, provides a basis and foundation for the construction of the multiple capital model so important for quantifying organizational information (Figure 2.8).

On top of including a variety of information and data, including operational and financial data, an underlying component of an integrated report is that it is meant to be both a historical reporting framework and a forward-looking tool. A critical flaw in the traditional financial reporting process is that it is exclusively focused on results and information that have already occurred. In order to effectively plan and succeed in a dynamic marketplace, however, management professionals must also be able to plan moving forward using the information available to them. An integrated reporting framework addresses this need by creating a strategic approach to how the information and data are both presented and communicated within the report. This addition of a strategic and forward-looking focus within this framework makes an integrated reporting framework a useful planning and forward-looking option, as well as a comprehensive analysis of current performance.

Flexibility, agility, and the ability to adapt in coordination with effective utilization of organizational information, appear to represent a set of competencies and competitive advantages for moving forward. Akin to how oil and other natural

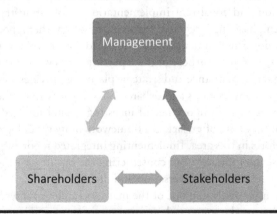

Figure 2.8 The relationship between management and the market.

resources provided the fuel and the resource foundation for prior generations of organizations to develop, grow, and succeed, information and data will provide the competitive advantage in a digitized and globally competitive landscape. Drilling down, and initiating a conversation that will be continued later throughout the book, in order to implement such a framework there are several changes and adjustments that must be made first prior to full implementation. In order to gather, analyze, collect, and report the wider variety of information necessary in an integrated report, information and control systems must also be updated and modified. Such an upgrade and differentiator is both another way in which integrated reporting stands apart from other frameworks and generates value to the management team.

These organizational changes and modifications that must be implemented prior to full adoption and utilization of an integrated reporting framework represent both a way in which this framework is differentiated and of the broader benefits generated through adoption of an integrated reporting framework. This also begins to answer a fundamentally important question—just what are the benefits of an integrated report?

What Are the Benefits of an Integrated Report?

When attempting to implement a new reporting framework, launch an initiative, or engage in any substantial changes to organizational policy, clear benefits and costs must be identified and analyzed. Particularly in a business environment that is multifaceted, frenetic, and involving an ever larger circle of stakeholders, the benefits of any additional initiative must be clear. Integrated reporting offers several benefits to organizations that choose to adopt this framework, and does so from an internal management and external user perspective. That said, it is important to remember that these benefits do not come without investments, resources, and the attention of management. Weighing these benefits versus the costs necessary to achieve and sustain these benefits is something every management team must perform in a logical and consistent manner.

This is a theme repeated throughout this book, and it is done so because it is so important to managing and growing a business that any new project or initiative must be in alignment with organizational objectives, both financial and operational. Making the business case, and avoiding the characterization that integrated reporting is simply another compliance-oriented requirement is an important part of making the case for integrated reporting. Illustrating and focusing on the potential benefits and opportunities associated with adopting an integrated reporting framework is a critical step toward achieving initial adoption and sustaining implementation over the medium to long term.

Articulating the business case and highlighting the upside and potential benefits of integrated reporting are important when making the case for implementation for internal stakeholders. While many of the external facing communications and dialogue around integrated reporting will be centered around external stakeholders and information delivered to end users, beginning this conversation from an internal perspective is important. Building support, making the investments necessary to upgrade technology and processes, and breaking down organizational silos are critical first steps. Especially when attempting to transition from traditional financial reporting to more comprehensive integrated reporting, it is important management are able to point to changes and initiatives already underway in other market leading organizations.

From an external reporting and communication framework, the benefits and upsides of implementing an integrated report are relatively straightforward to understand. First, a more strategic and forward-looking reporting framework provides much needed information and clarification for stakeholders seeking to evaluate the current and projected performance of the organization. Shareholders and stakeholders alike are, rather obviously, interested in what the management team has planned for moving forward, and creating a reporting structure to fulfill these expectations makes logical sense. Additionally, another benefit from an external reporting and data perspective is that reporting these different varieties of information, via the multiple capital model, provides users with important information for analytic purposes. For example, including information and metrics about intellectual capital for an entertainment company makes logical sense.

One prominent example of just how important this type of reporting could be for entertainment purposes was demonstrated in the late 2017 proposed acquisition of Fox assets by Disney. The overarching driving forces behind this over $50 billion acquisition were the intellectual assets and property under the umbrella of Fox, which primarily focused on emerging and international markets. Rights to movies and other organizational assets provided Disney with much needed international initiatives and expansion possibilities in the face of growing competition from organizations like Amazon and Netflix. Documenting and reporting the types of information and data linked to intellectual capital and property provided management and external shareholders with much needed quantitative information to analyze this transaction.

Internal Benefits

On top of the benefits to external stakeholders and shareholders through a more comprehensive and holistic template and model of reporting, there are benefits attributable to internal users as well. Reporting different types and classes of information, organizing this information into a quantitative format, and doing so in a consistent manner necessitates several changes and modifications to internal processes and controls. Building on the increased digitization of operations across different industry lines, including the IoT that dominates many organizational processes, management professionals are awash in large amounts of data. Harnessing this information for the purpose of an integrated reporting framework requires integrating data and data-based decision-making for every decision made at the strategic level. Increases in training, education, and an investment in resources to upgrade and modify existing information systems are required to both implement an integrated reporting framework and to generate ancillary benefits for employees of the firm.

Making action-oriented decisions is the prerogative, along with generating stakeholder value, of management professionals and teams across different industry lines. Information technology and increased data management represent competencies and expertise that are equally in high demand, but that also require training and education in an increasingly digitized marketplace. By leveraging the investments already underway in various technology and analytical platforms organizations can, and should, be taking proactive steps to harness and leverage the different varieties of information available to them. Implementing an integrated reporting framework requires both a change in mindset and a quantitative change in how organizations collect, analyze, and report information. In order to fulfill the varied expectations of the numerous stakeholder groups interested in how the organization is performing requires management to engage in a variety of changes internally. That said, merely investing financial resources will be insufficient to generate the types of changes required to fulfill and even exceed the needs and expectations of stakeholders—a more comprehensive approach is required.

Integrating different types and forms of information into the financial reporting and communication process is an increasingly expected approach and mindset for management professionals to adopt across industry lines. This shift in approach to both internal and external reporting will impress upon on employees throughout the organization the importance of data integrity, of collecting this information, and of linking operational results to financial reporting. Linking these different types of information to a more comprehensive reporting framework is not only integral to the success of implementing an integrated reporting framework, but also necessary to fulfill stakeholder expectations. In order to do so, however, employees in the organization—and not only senior leadership—must embrace and understand the implications of operational information on the performance of the firm. Such an approach, and change in mindset represents a fundamental shift in how many organizations operate currently, in a siloed approach where different employees focus on different subsets of data.

This shift in mindset, realizing that different types of information must be coalesced and reported in a manner both meaningful and timely for stakeholder groups, cannot be underestimated. Changing the orientation and internal processes of a wide array of employees, from senior leadership to front line employees, is one of the most dynamic benefits of adopting an integrated reporting framework. In a digitally oriented and motivated environment competitive both on a domestic and international landscape, developing a holistic and comprehensive communication system is critically important. The need and expectation of a comprehensive view of performance fulfills a need from a financial management and corporate governance perspective. Moving forward, it is important to take into account that an integrated reporting framework helps management professionals meet governance expectations, shareholder expectations, and human resources development goals. This circular cycle of benefits and connection to the idea of intellectual property and capital also represents an ancillary benefit from the adoption of such a reporting framework.

Chapter 3

The Current State of Integrated Reporting: Applications and Insights

As practitioners and researchers attempt to compare integrated reporting versus other nonfinancial frameworks already in existence, in addition to the rapid technological changes underway within the profession, the practical applications and insights embedded in an integrated reporting framework are important to emphasize and illustrate. For management professionals already juggling expectations and requirements from a variety of internal and external groups, insights and benefits must be connected. Data drive business decision-making, and the insights potentially gleaned from different sources of information can be the difference between success or failure in a rapidly moving business environment.

The International Integrated Reporting Council: Information and Resources

Analyzing the current state of integrated reporting requires analyzing both the institutional support embodied by the international integrated reporting council (IIRC), other professional associations, and actions underway by members of the business community. Specifically, the IIRC has put together several sources of information for the purposes of research and for consultation by management to evaluate the impact of integrated reporting on current business models. Recognizing the impact of integrated reporting on both a strategic and operational level, it is also worth noting that the adoption of an integrated reporting framework spans multiple industry lines, and includes participants not traditionally associated with environmental or sustainability reporting. Historically, environmental reporting, sustainability reporting, or other types of nonfinancial information have focused on organizations already operating in these areas, but integrated reporting generates a platform applicable to virtually any organization. Generating better insights, leveraging the increased availability of information within organizations, and using this data to make the best use of organizational resources represent trends which cross industry lines. That said, there is an interesting trend worth noting prior to drilling into some examples of integrated reporting adoption.

Reporting and analyzing an organization from a comprehensive and holistic point of view is something that would, on its surface, be appealing to organizations and management professionals, regardless of geographic location or base of operations. Interestingly, and perhaps more a reflection of historical trends rather than current market realities and opinions, integrated financial reporting has taken off and obtained leading market share positions both in Japan and Western Europe compared to the United States. Even more prominent, is the requirement in South Africa that all publicly listed companies in Johannesburg report information using an integrated reporting framework. These adoptions, specifically in Western Europe and Japan, may reflect more the mindset of management and corporate governance than an overt focus on sustainability and environmental issues.

Contrasting the shareholder view of management responsibility and fiduciary duty most commonly found in the United States as the prerogative of organizations, different corporate governance methodologies exist in other markets. Western European organizations, for example, maintain seats on the board level for representatives of employees, labor organizations, and other constituency groups. Such inclusion not only focuses the attention and energy of the organization, and senior leadership, on a broader array of areas versus quarterly earnings reports, but additional benefits are generated. Including such a variety of stakeholder groups at the highest level of decision-making also makes it more likely the organization will plan and strategize for the longer term. Such engagement and dialogue is not a guarantee of organizational success in the medium and long term, nor of ethical operations—as demonstrated by high profile failures in organization such as Volkswagen, nevertheless it is interesting to examine this linkage. By onboarding a broader array of stakeholder groups and integrating these disparate points of view into the strategic decision-making process, an evolution and transition toward integrated reporting is a logical extension of this topic.

Corporate operations and management in Japan, similar in nature to the broader base of reporting and performance reported by Western European organizations, tend to emphasize additional information on top of pure financial performance. Specifically, corporate culture, employer and employee loyalty, and a commitment to long-term planning form a core structure of Japanese management philosophy. This longer-term focus, emphasis on employee retention and training, and subordination of financial information versus other reporting factors creates an environment hospitable to an integrated reporting framework. With over 300 major corporations listed in Japan utilizing an integrated reporting framework, Japan is an excellent market for further analysis and research in the area of integrated reporting and associated financial effects. Interestingly, however, as stakeholder pressures and forces become increasingly evident and present, the integration and implementation of integrated reporting and other nonfinancial reporting frameworks is occurring with more frequency in the broader marketplace.

As of this writing there are organizations in virtually every industry utilizing an integrated financial reporting framework to assist in the clarification and communication of information and insights to both internal and external stakeholders seeking information on organizational performance. The organizational and industry specific driving forces will inevitably differ from firm to firm, but it is important to acknowledge the reality that nonfinancial data influence how decisions are made across industry lines. Focusing on this reality, we take into account the variety of forces influencing decision-making, which are more alike than they are differentiated in a business environment increasingly interconnected and dynamic.

Connecting Integrated Reporting to Other Forces

It would be simple but incorrect to correlate integrated financial reporting with other types of sustainability and nonfinancial reporting. While such a connection and linkage does appear to exist because an integrated report does include sustainability information, there are numerous other components within an integrated report that do not exist in other frameworks. Circling back to the core value proposition of integrated reporting, a quantitative framework reporting financial and nonfinancial data to external decision makers differentiates integrated reporting from existing sustainability reporting. Numerous organizations report sustainability information, and some even do so in a quantitative and consistent manner, but all too often this data is reported on a standalone basis. This lack of integration and combination with other types and streams of information means there is a lack of cohesiveness and comparability with this type of reporting.

An associated benefit of this increased cohesion and consistency with regard to different types of nonfinancial information is that end users of this data will be able to rely more effectively on this information. A key benefit and upside of traditional financial information, and the reporting frameworks built up around this traditional financial information, is that end users are familiar with both the information and associated implications. Nonfinancial information and data, even though it is what inevitably drives the financial performance of the organization is not as consistent nor as standardized as financial information. Every organization, management team, and end user that receive this information understands what net income represents, how to differentiate cash flow from other financial metrics, and how to analyze a balance sheet. Regardless of industry specificity, opinion of management, or geographic location of business operations financial statements must be issued in a comparable and consistent format.

This fundamental difference has been a stumbling block for other previous nonfinancial reporting frameworks. Involving financial and accounting professionals will help create increased standards and consistency in the reporting environment, increase the understandability of information, and generate an additional upside that may have been overlooked until now. Increasing the standardization and transparency around nonfinancial information also opens the door for increased assurance and auditing standards. The importance of auditing and generating additional assurance standards and reports around nonfinancial information is important, both for internal and external users of information. By increasing the reliability of information, clarifying gaps in understanding and reliability of nonfinancial information, and increasing standardization in this area the reliability and usability of this information increases as well.

Sustainability reporting clearly provides benefits and information to interested stakeholder groups, especially nongovernmental and environmental organizations; however, this by itself replicates an existing problem. Traditional financial reporting, as is often documented, is only appealing to a very narrow set of end users, namely creditors and shareholders due to the focused nature of this information. Different types of sustainability reporting, whether they are oriented toward quantifying the impact of carbon emissions, water discharge, replenishment, or other restoration initiatives will only be interesting and useful toward a narrow set of users. Contrasting with this format and view, an integrated financial report is by its very nature a more comprehensive and holistic reporting framework integrating a variety of types of information. Specifically, through the expansion of sustainability reporting via an integrated report comes the ability of management professionals to treat sustainability projects like a financial portfolio.

Evaluating sustainability projects, via a reporting framework, like an assortment of financial projects may seem counterintuitive upon initial review. An argument is often made that in the context of sustainability reporting and sustainability information, financial results should not be the primary consideration. This situation, however, creates an environment in which management professionals are aware that financial professionals do not always consider sustainability initiatives as mission-oriented. Such a dynamic is unhealthy, both in the short term from a management perspective and in the longer-term likelihood that sustainability projects will be integrated into continuing business operations. That said, taking into account the financial implications of sustainability projects and initiatives is an imperative part of making sustainability a permanent part of the C-suite conversation. One example of how to evaluate projects that integrate both environmental and financial impact is how Adidas manages a variety of sustainability projects. Clearly, every organization is different, but this example provides a possible path as to how management teams can evolve from current reporting and build a bridge to a more integrated reporting framework.

Adidas Case Study

Managing sustainability projects, especially in a business environment with record low interest rates, is a challenge for management professionals seeking to generate sufficient business returns. As a counterbalance to the requirement for investment and business returns, organizations and management professionals must also be wary of engaging in greenwashing activities. Greenwashing activities have been a focal topic of the sustainability management and reporting process since its inception, and does not directly benefit either internal management decision makers nor external shareholders. Examples of such activities include launching sustainability initiatives or projects without sufficient funding, using platitudes to wash over the reality that underlying changes are not underway and sustainability activities are not linked to the underlying business operations. Regardless of in which category greenwashing activities may fall, the reality is that without an effective quantitative format to rank and evaluate sustainability projects the possibility of greenwashing will continue to exist (Figure 3.1).

Adidas, a large multinational corporation, offers a concrete example of how sustainability can be integrated into ongoing business operations while dovetailing with an integrated reporting framework. Coordinating with the environmental defense fund (EDF), Adidas launched a training and management development program seeking to more effectively quantify and analyze the financial impacts of sustainability activities. Mirroring the initiatives launched by fellow retail and apparel maker Puma, namely Life Cycle Accounting, Adidas was attempting to effectively integrate sustainability within the reporting process. Specifically, and

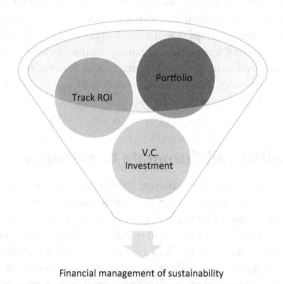

Financial management of sustainability

Figure 3.1   Adidas case study of sustainability.

drilling down to the actions underway by Adidas, the management team framed sustainability in the context of a portfolio investment. Taking this approach generates several benefits that can be replicated across industry and organizational lines, even for those who have more limited resources than Adidas.

First, treating sustainability projects and initiatives like—for lack of a better word—any other initiatives communicates a clear message to both internal and external users. Time and again the importance of communication cannot be overstated when it pertains to implementing an integrated financial report. Linking the operational and financial benefits of sustainability within the existing reporting framework is important in engendering management support and sustainability for the initiative over the long term. Second, analyzing the financial implications and effects of sustainability projects on the bottom line of an organization requires that management quantitatively track and evaluate just how these projects are performing. As the adage goes, what is measured is what is truly managed, and this rings equally true when it pertains to sustainability data and reporting. Building a bridge between initiatives launched with an environmental slant and their financial impact is also an approach mirrored within the integrated reporting framework.

Third, and perhaps most importantly for implementing integrated reporting, this information is reported in an integrated and comprehensive manner within the broader scope of how Adidas performs overall. Specifically, this allows more financially successful projects to offset and help subsidize projects and initiatives which might not be able to financially survive exclusively on their own. While every project and idea engaged in by the organization should be able to eventually justify itself on its own merits, some projects may have a longer payoff period or result in qualitative benefits versus strictly quantitative benefits. Organizing the results of said projects and ideas in a quantitative format, and taking into account the idea that some financially successful projects will offset less initially profitable ideas also links to an integrated reporting framework. Quantifying the financial impact and results of environmentally and sustainability oriented projects ties directly to the concept of natural capital; however, this is not the only reporting initiative supporting and reinforcing the idea of an integrated report.

Human Capital and Corporate Governance

The ideas of human capital and corporate governance are not unique to either the integrated reporting conversation nor the postfinancial crisis market. Thus, it is important to keep in mind that the concepts linked to human capital and corporate governance have been involved in decision-making for decades, and continue to have a powerful influence on how organizations are managed both domestically and abroad. Human capital, linking back to the concepts discussed previously, is an essential component of how management professionals develop and grow a company over the medium and long term. Corporate governance, upon initial review, may seem to represent an abstract and ethereal type of concept, but is actually an idea and important construct integrated into every aspect of the organization. Building a bridge to connect the concepts of human capital and corporate governance is an increasingly prevalent trend in the marketplace, and an idea embedded within the multiple capital model.

Corporate governance, at the most basic level, represents the interactions between the board of directors and management on an internal basis, as well as the interaction the organization has with external stakeholders. While there is a great deal of communication about how important it is for organizations to keep different stakeholder and shareholder groups involved and integrated into the decision-making process, quantifying these efforts is an area where there remains room for improvement. Especially as the business landscape and environment continue to evolve and diversify in a rapidly expanding manner, interactions between different stakeholder groups will only have a larger impact on how decisions are made moving forward. Building on these concepts, and further integrating these different types of information into how management professionals make certain decisions is virtually embedded into the integrated reporting framework. Embracing a broader stakeholder landscape and the associated implications of this diversified stakeholder base is the quantitative link management professionals increasingly look for in the global business landscape.

Quantifying the impact of corporate governance on how organizations and management teams make decisions, and weaving these impacts into the integrated reporting framework is a key feature of integrated reporting. These different types of information can be summarized, while also drilling down to the specific implications of corporate governance, in the form of activist investors. Particularly as management professionals seek to implement a more comprehensive and holistic view of reporting and management throughout the firm, it is inevitable that some financial shareholders might raise questions. Analyzing the veracity and worthwhileness of an integrated report is not a negative event; frankly, any idea or strategy embraced by management should be critically examined.

Integrated Reporting and Corporate Governance

Corporate governance is an idea and concept which, somewhat unfortunately, has traditionally been associated with qualitative decision-making focused in the hands of both the Board of Directors and senior management. Such a mindset and approach, which generate some benefits in terms of strategy planning and substantial investment choices, are not agile or flexible enough in the current business landscape. News events of a significant nature, both positive and negative, can occur nearly instantaneously— management teams must be nimble enough to respond effectively. Perhaps more significantly, as illustrated by the success of organizations that have embraced a longer-term perspective, is the fact that focusing on longer-term growth is accretive to financial and nonfinancial stakeholders. One relatively recent example in the American business landscape was the transaction that resulted in Dell transitioning from a publicly traded firm to one privately held and operated. While there were clearly competitive and other business reasons for this transaction, one item often reported was that going private provided management with additional flexibility.

Instead of simply going private, usually via a management-led repurchase of shares, which can be an expensive and complicated way of removing the organization from the public market and associated scrutiny, a more robust and comprehensive way of documenting and reporting governance projects can add value to management. Simply by providing management teams with a framework, reports, and dashboards with which to communicate strategic information to stakeholders, organizations can get in front of a number of potentially challenging issues. Circling back to the format and template of an integrated report demonstrates this clear connection. Management professionals, under pressure from a variety of institutional investors, are paying increasing amounts of attention to environmental, sustainability, and governance issues at a strategic level. Even with this focus, however, shareholders expect to see some sort of justification for engaging in these initiatives.

A key responsibility of management professionals, in addition to the fiduciary duty for maximizing the financial performance of the organization, is to do so in a sustainable manner over the long term. These two mindsets, however, can often result in mixed messages, clashing investment strategies, and a muddled sense of just what the strategy of the organization is. Communication, explanation, and the construction of a narrative around the ideas put forth by management are something that cannot be overlooked as a benefit of an integrated report. Human capital is clearly a part of the management decision-making process, and the intersection of corporate governance, human capital, and increased transparency is a critical shift moving forward as management professionals seek to report financial and nonfinancial information to a wide variety of stakeholders. An open-ended question, however, is just how to gather and quantify these different varieties of information—the status quo is insufficient.

Better Data and Analytics

One of the underlying fundamental truths about an integrated report is that this reporting framework contains a much larger variety of information and data than traditional reporting. This broader variety of information is a strength of the integrated reporting framework, but also represents a challenge for organizations seeking to implement such a framework. Simply put, and contrasting with the singular amount and type of information normally reported to stakeholders, management must be able to harness different streams of data on a continuous basis. This realization also leads to the fact that, in virtually every case, that organizations must invest in additional training and resources to keep pace with the increasing needs for data by different stakeholder groups. It is important to note, however, that simply investing financial resources is insufficient, and that education and training, as well as selecting specific tools relevant for their company are critically important.

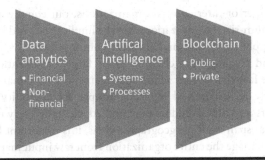

Figure 3.2   The evolution of blockchain technology.

Cutting through the clutter and various types of information and tools available there appear to be two trends and technologies particularly relevant for collecting data and enabling continuous reporting (Figure 3.2).

Blockchain technology has received a tremendous amount of media coverage and analysis especially as viewed through the lens of Bitcoin technology; however, the implication of this tool is much broader than simply one specific cryptocurrency. At the core of this technology is a decentralized computing network that enables organizations to track, report, and analyze virtually any kind of information an organization would have at its disposal. The specifics of this technology and platform are less important for our purposes than what the implications of using this tool are on the data reporting and analysis processes of an organization. A key benefit of blockchain to facilitate the adoption of a more comprehensive and integrative reporting process is the real-time nature of data verification. Taking a step back, and without diving too much into the technical details of how a blockchain network would operate, let's take a look at the fundamentals which make continuous reporting possible.

At the core of blockchain is the blockchain network, which consists of computers or servers (labeled as nodes) connected or signed into the blockchain. Assuming that this blockchain is a corporate blockchain, or a network that connects an organization with its suppliers and partners, the following benefits can almost immediately be realized: (1) by connecting to the network, every organization must be initially verified and identified by every other party already present in the network; and (2) after the various organizations have been added to the network, every organization in the network has real-time access to every single transaction and point of data in the network. For example, the vendors and suppliers that are part of the blockchain will be able to verify supply chain information on a continuous basis.

Supply Chain Implications

Analysts would be hard-pressed to find a component of business management and operations more integrated throughout business operations than supply chains.

Especially for larger or international organizations, but equally as applicable for smaller and medium-sized organizations, are the implications and linkages between pieces of the supply chain and management communication. One aspect in the sustainability and responsibility chain at many larger organizations that may be overlooked is the fact that even if senior management at headquarters, or at offices located in highly industrialized markets, adopts sustainability initiatives and projects, suppliers and other vendors may not. As virtually every organization has supply chains that span multiple geographic areas, it is important for management professionals to manage the entire organization from raw input materials to finished products.

A fundamental issue in any supply chain that spans and includes multiple organizations is that, even with additional sensors and information available to management decision makers, there are large gaps in information tracking and reporting. For example, of particular importance for organizations inputting portions or entire goods from international suppliers and producers is that certain goods and services may not be assembled in compliance with environmental or labor standards. In addition to the environmental or human damage caused by these activities, there is the real possibility that due to these mixed messages and performances the strategy of the organization is disrupted and potentially derailed. Leveraging advances in technology, specifically the opportunities from blockchain technology, provides management with an action-oriented path to solidify supply chain relationships and improve supply chain strength.

For example, imagine an organization operating in the quick service restaurant industry having operations in multiple locations and suppliers in other areas as well. This may sound like an issue only applicable for the largest multinational organizations but even firms operating in large continuous geographic areas (such as the United States) can present significant logistical issues. Gathering, washing, and shipping different types of food input materials from these different areas present a number of opportunities for breaches of quality control, sanitation, environmental, and employee standards. As stakeholders and customers increasingly inquire about just how food is prepared and served, remaining aware of this information is not an idle or theoretical issue. Installing different types of computerized sensors and platforms at different points throughout the process will, of course, alleviate some of the information asymmetry embedded in this situation. That said even with sensors and other detective computerized systems in place throughout the organization, the ability to access this information in real time is still wanting. Especially if a management team is attempting to implement an integrated report—complete with a more forward-looking and strategic aspects of the reporting process—this information must be available in real time.

Blockchain technology, using many of the benefits of a distributed ledger platform, allows all partners and involved organizations access to this information in a continuous manner and in real time. Integrating these flows of information, especially when available in a real-time and accessible manner to all participants, allows pain points and pressure areas to be identified and alleviated almost as quickly as they arise. An additional benefit and attribute related to the implementation of blockchain and supply chains is that, by the virtue of the blockchain technology platform itself, data and transactions are encrypted and secured against hacks, breaches, and other such incidents. Building on the already increasing rate of data integration and analysis taking place throughout the decision-making process, the implications of blockchain for integrated reporting are clear.

Integrated Reporting and the Status Quo

Integrated reporting, by virtue of the types of information and data embedded and included in the reporting template, requires management to make investments and decisions linked to emerging technologies and analytics. In order to successfully implement a blockchain paradigm within an organization, the management team cannot simply place blockchain protocols into effect without transitioning and changing the underlying business processes throughout the firm. Digitization is having a dramatic impact on business practices, communication protocols, and stakeholder engagement throughout the organization, and is also directly connected to the changing status quo in the business landscape. Put simply, the status quo as it relates to technology, reporting, and organizational analytics will be insufficiently moving forward. Management practices, reporting paradigms, and the crafting of organizational strategy will be influenced by the growing variety of data both available to decision makers and expected by stakeholders. Quantifying, analyzing, and reporting these different changes as they relate to the status quo of the how organizations are managed is an important step in implementing.

Drilling down into the adoption process of integrated reporting it is important to circle back to the challenges facing a variety of organizations. Stakeholder groups, including financial and nonfinancial entities, are interested in not only how the organization is currently performing, but also how sustainable this rate of performance is over the medium and long term. In order to meet these expectations, management professionals are seeking to differentiate themselves through better performance and information disclosure. Engaging in more proactive and comprehensive disclosure and reporting, however, is not something that can be done with current tools and processes—a new paradigm is required. Integrated reporting, as outlined in these previous pages, clearly has the potential to serve as a foundation from which more holistic and comprehensive reporting is possible. Even with adoption already underway, however, it is important to acknowledge that external leadership and support is necessary.

It is important to note that an organization need not completely pivot or transition from a traditional reporting framework to a fully integrated framework all at once, and that the transition period will differ from organization to organization. The importance of nonfinancial information does not appear to be positioned to overtake that of financial performance, but the reality is both sets of data are important for organizational success. In such an environment, where many organizations are in flux and at different stages of adoption, leveraging external guidance and information to enact the available best practices appears to make good business sense. Professional advocacy and information produced by professional organizations can lend much needed objectivity and clarification to questions, concerns, and other issues inevitably arising. Additionally, and depending on the specific industry or industry subset the organization is involved in, the technical details and reporting information can be complicated and need additional clarification.

Prior to delving into some of the examples of professional advocacy and support already in existence in the marketplace, it is logical to analyze why such support is important. Particular organizations and management professionals, regardless of industry affiliation or subsets of interest, always possess some kind of bias or interest. This is, in and of itself, neither a positive or negative development but is something which can be viewed more or less negatively by groups of external stakeholders. Specifically, if the adoption of a longer-term mindset results in subpar performance from a financial perspective, critiques will be leveled against the management team in charge. This is just one reason why professional associations supporting and advocating these mindsets, approaches, and paradigm shifts are so important. Such support adds validity and objectivity to the conversation and adoption of such tools by larger swaths of the marketplace.

Financial Impact of ESG and Other Nonfinancial Information

Taking a high level approach and examining the various qualitative factors and forces influencing the greater adoption of integrated reporting and other nonfinancial reporting are not enough to create a viable business case. In order to facilitate and create a true business case and to discuss with management and external stakeholders, a quantitative connection between integrated reporting and financial performance must be constructed. The reality is—no matter how long-term or holistic in mindset a specific group of management professionals are—the specter of short-term financial performance is a trend and force impossible to ignore. Taking this into account, integrating these different forces into a comprehensive reporting and communication structure, and producing said information on a continuous basis require both support from management and a financial underpinning for these various initiatives.

Nonfinancial information is an umbrella encompassing a wide array of data and data sets, which can sometimes make it difficult to establish and enforce standard metrics for reporting information. Some organizations, including both Coca-Cola and Adidas, have begun to quantify, report, and distribute information connected to internal operations and process. Additionally, standard setting bodies and groups including the SASB and GRI framework offer some guidance and information, which can be used to help quantify these different streams of information in a consistent manner. That said it is important to link together the different streams of operational information with financial performance, and to also connect the impact nonfinancial information has on financial outcomes, performance, and rankings in the marketplace. As if this task was not challenging enough, not every financial metric or performance indicator is equally as applicable for every organization. For example, market-leading organizations, including the high profile example of Amazon, may not achieve consistent profitability across different business segments and lines.

One of the most widely used metrics and tactics among financial analysts, internal users, and other external users of organizational information is the market capitalization of the organization in question. While the mathematical calculation for market capitalization simply involves the current share price times the outstanding number of shares, the implication and ripple effects of this metric are felt throughout the business decision-making process. For example, organizations and the associated management professionals tasked with leading the organization are often judged by not only how the firm performs on an earnings per share or income basis, but additionally the long-term valuation of the organization is also of great interest to internal and external stakeholders. Specifically, bridging the gap and connecting the dots between information produced internally by the organization and the resulting effect these items have on the market capitalization of the organization will have implications on both the short-term performance of the organization and the long-term success of the entity moving forward.

Obtaining a quantitative basis for comparison and analysis, however, may be difficult to gather given the debate and ongoing conversation around the importance and validity of nonfinancial information. Drilling down, the market capitalization of the organization appears to offer a valid path forward in not only ascertaining the value of the organization, but also the value of intangible and other nonfinancial assets. Even with market volatility, including upward trends and downward movements, the value of an organization may lie in additional information that builds upon the information and data contained in a traditional financial report. Applying this in a practical sense requires that organizations and management professionals incorporate nonfinancial information in a financial reporting construct and connect this information to the value of the corporation in the marketplace. Identifying the specific methodologies in place will result in both a comprehensive analysis of how the organization performs and how this information connects to the medium and long-term performance of the organization. While it is clear that market valuation may increase or decrease over time and be subject to short-term volatility, intangible assets account for an increasing percentage of organizational valuation.

Chapter 4

Leaders and Support for Integrated Reporting

From a practical point of view, it is nearly impossible to begin the adoption and implementation of a comprehensive shift in reporting and analyzing information without examining and discussing leading organizations. It is logical to analyze and build off of the work already underway at market leading organizations, especially in an area of emerging importance such as integrated reporting. Clearly, many of the leading insights and applications of integrated reporting appear to represent larger and more established organizations, but it does not mean that the attributes and insights gleaned from integrated reporting may not be equally applicable to organizations of every size. Regardless of where the adoption and implementation progress begins, or if the integrated reporting is rolled out over a period of time, the underlying mission is more important than the pace of adoption. In addition to the market support and evidence presented by the organizations that have either adopted integrated reporting or are starting the process of reporting nonfinancial information, leveraging publicly available data and information such as produced by the IIRC provides management much needed guidance and advice to propel this effort forward. Chapter 4 highlights the market evidence linked to integrated reporting and also what external resources are also available.

The adoption of integrated financial reporting by organizations across the globe clearly demonstrates the importance and business case for such a reporting framework. Engaging financial and nonfinancial stakeholders is emerging as a critical management challenge for professionals across industry lines. Different organizations will clearly have varying specific prerogatives, but the trend toward more comprehensive reporting is readily apparent. Inherent biases must be taken into account particularly in a business environment where media, and specifically social media, can influence and drive the fortunes of an organization in a nearly instantaneous manner. In other words, and through no fault of management involved nor with any negative connotation implied, every organization and management professional has certain metrics and types of information that take priority over other types of information. This is where the support of an unaffiliated third party, and one that is already involved in the accounting and financial profession at large, is invaluable for successfully implementing integrated reporting on a broad basis.

The International Integrated Reporting Council (IIRC) is a logical place to begin the analysis of third-party advocacy support of integrated reporting on a global basis. Although a substantial percentage of the organizations initially adopting integrated reporting were based in Europe—and this initial burst of enthusiasm was reflected in the composition and focus of the IIRC, the organization has made significant progress toward a more global approach. Specifically, the IIRC has organized its various advocacy efforts into several distinct areas, differentiated by the practitioners, academics, or investors targeted for engagement in these efforts. The IIRC has provided access to examples and case studies of successful implementation, publishing and distributing reports on a consistent basis reflecting the progress of integrated reporting.

Connecting back to the possibly more comprehensive board and director membership of European organizations, the fact that the IIRC came into existence on the European continent does not seem entirely illogical. While these efforts may have initially begun in Europe, the adoption and implementation of integrated reporting has spread to numerous different markets across geographic and political lines. Such adoption, even between different marketplaces and governmental actors who may not see eye to eye on virtually any other issue, seems to indicate just how widespread the support is for a more comprehensive reporting and communication structure. Even more beneficial for adopters of integrated reporting is that the IIRC provides additional background, data, and contextual guidance for management professionals seeking to implement such a framework.

The IIRC currently provides an integrated reporting examples database for organizations, academics, and investors to refer to, draw from, and make use of. It also links to the underlying concept of thought leadership in this area. Virtually by the nature of integrated reporting itself, the idea of a more comprehensive reporting structure and framework there is an embedded nature of thought leadership and forward thinking management involved. Stated another way, since the integrated reporting framework requires the quantification and reporting of larger varieties of information, management professionals must use a more comprehensive view of how the organization is actually performing. This more holistic view of organizational performance also links back to the growing importance of different stakeholder groups, all equally interested in the performance of the organization, and the increasing availability of information provides management with the ability of fulfill these multifaceted objectives. Even with this internationally based support, however, it is important especially for external users to take into account the impact that accounting specific guidance and regulations can have on the reporting process. Furthermore, the Association of International Certified Professionals Accountants (AICPA) and the Institute of Management Accountants (IMA) provide examples of thought leadership and research from an accounting perspective; as such, promoting integrated reporting is a directive readily apparent throughout these organizations.

The AICPA and IMA have both adapted to the changing business landscape following the financial crisis of 2007–2008 and have launched a bevy of initiatives. Focusing on areas such as cybersecurity, providing assurance to data and security systems, and creating reports on nonfinancial information and data are included in these developments. Linking back to the concept of integrated reporting, the validity and credibility granted by these organizations to this process is difficult to overstate for management professionals. Both organizations combined, although appealing to and serving different subsets of the accounting profession, have hundreds of thousands of members and a global reach. An important first step toward more widespread adoption and utilization of integrated reporting is the buy-in of accounting professionals tasked with preparing and reporting this information. Additionally, and arguably more important from the perspective of implementation is the reality that greater standardization and consistency are required in this area. The increasing support for nonfinancial and more comprehensive reporting by these organizations provides a foundation for this conversation and development to occur.

Integrated Reporting and Transparency

In a business environment increasingly dominated by intellectual property, intangible assets, and the importance of maintaining trade secrets to form competitive advantages, it is equally important to recognize the importance of being transparent and forthcoming with other types of information. Specifically, while it certainly is understandable and reasonable to expect certain data, such as patents or confidential intellectual property, to remain proprietary, sustainability and other environmental information are of interest to an ever-increasing number of stakeholders. Transparency, while not directly correlated to innovation and business growth, is a factor that plays a definitive role in many third-party business indices, rankings, and listings of countries determining the ease of doing business in a certain area. It is true that transparency is easier to achieve via different technology platforms in the modern era of social media and communication platforms, but it still requires a concerted effort on the part of management professionals to transform this desire for transparency into action.

Leveraging an integrated reporting platform, especially when taking into account the changes already impacting the business environment at large, also requires that management professionals acknowledge the growing importance of transparency for ongoing business operations. Transparency, however, means much more than simply reporting the current results of business operations; in a globalized business environment it increasingly requires that organizations inform stakeholders of projected plans and future strategy as in addition to analyzing current results. Communicating and interacting with stakeholders, including financial and nonfinancial stakeholders, is both a fiduciary responsibility of management and also a method by which the organization can deliver and create value in a competitive landscape. However, transparency without organization and methodology is simply another reporting obligation placed upon organizations and management professionals without a definitive upside or benefit.

Information and communicating this information to different stakeholder groups provides one of the key benefits of integrated reporting and a definitive method by which organizations can illustrate and highlight the value of different strategic initiatives underway at the organization. Building this bridge and connecting short-term performance and longer-term financial performance represents a key differentiating factor in a business landscape increasingly interested in not only how organizations perform, but how these results are achieved. Supported by the multiple capital model (which includes financial capital plus an additional five definitions of capital for external stakeholders), integrated reporting provides a vehicle to achieve both the goal of increased information communication and a better-informed stakeholder base. Examining the business landscape, in addition to providing real-world examples of how integrated reporting has been implemented, also provides management professionals with evidence of how this tool can be applied across various industry lines.

Benefit Corporations

Benefit corporations may seem like a contradictory or seemingly incongruous methodology for reporting the results and information of financial information. That said, the development, increased coverage, and growing utilization of the b-corp framework and mindset provides additional background and foundational information for organizations interested in integrated reporting. Prior to connecting the thread of information and data between benefit corporations and integrated reporting, it is important to analyze what exactly benefit corporations represent. At a high level, the information and ideas of benefit corporations require that organizations and management professionals embed and include the nonfinancial data alongside financial information within articles of incorporation, periodic reports, and communication to stakeholders. Connecting the different types of information, and illustrating the fact that management places nonfinancial and financial information on an equal footing is an important step toward ensuring both realistic reporting and management actions.

An important first step in the process of integrating nonfinancial data into the framework and pipeline of data communicated to internal and external users is to embed these sources of data into the core of how management operates the business.

This is usually constituted and completed by the highest level of the organization including the board and senior management levels, connecting and highlighting the importance of sustainability and other applicable nonfinancial information into what drives the organization forward. It is difficult to overstate just how important it is for organizations to connect different types of information, and weave them into how performance is communicated. Drilling down, this fact and the direct connection between financial and nonfinancial goals provide several benefits to management professionals, the organization as a whole, and the customers/clients serviced by the firm.

First, by embedding and connecting the financial and operational goals of the organization there is a clear communication of where the organization is going and what tactics and ideas will be used by the firm, as well as the importance of nonfinancial information to the success of the organization. This is an important point to acknowledge, because even if an organization advocates and supports the inclusion of nonfinancial information, it is entirely different to enshrine these values and information into the articles of incorporation. On top of the communicative benefit of taking such actions, it is also realistic to recognize the fact that this high level importance also can generate changes in reporting and other internal processes within the firm. Put simply, beginning the inclusion and highlighting the importance placing statements and nonfinancial information at the board and senior management level can lead to fundamental changes in how data is analyzed and reported to stakeholders.

Second, and building on the first benefit, this means that since organizations and management professionals are tasked with reporting, documenting, and managing the various streams of nonfinancial data produced by the organization, the internal systems and processes of the organization must align around these objectives. Specifically, and connecting almost directly to a fully integrated reporting framework are the metrics, tools, and reports generated by tracking and analyzing both financial and nonfinancial information. This includes, but is not limited to the accounting and finance metrics, and may also include new metrics and reporting tools for quantifying nonfinancial information. As processes and different procedures are developed and built out throughout the firm, internal and external stakeholders have access to not only larger amounts of information, but also have access to reports tracking associated performance. Development and reinforcement of consistent reporting standards, frameworks, and other tools are not only a necessity in a stakeholder environment but also add additional transparency to how the organization is performing for interested parties. Such transparency also allows management teams to highlight the benefits and the forward-looking nature of strategies underway in an organization, as well as connecting strategic plans to both financial and nonfinancial goals.

Third, and arguably the most important benefit for organizations and management teams seeking to leverage the increased interest in comprehensive performance is to operate the business for success in over the medium and long term, instead of being managed exclusively around short term financial metrics. The ability to invest, make decisions, and launch initiatives to build value in a comprehensive and holistic manner is a strategy that would appear to set an organization apart from competition. No business exists in a vacuum, and while this fact is widely acknowledged and treated as commonsense knowledge, making this reality part of a business strategy represents an important next step. Benefit corporations are rapidly expanding both in numbers and the scope of industries covered, illustrating the benefits that can be accrued to different organizations over certain periods of time. It is also realistic to recognize the fact that by embedding nonfinancial metrics and goals, management and external stakeholders are more likely to see eye to eye on managerial decision-making.

It is important to acknowledge the reality that greenwashing, highlighting certain initiatives at the expense of other projects, and not walking the proverbial walk represent risks to any such initiative or project. An important item to remember and keep in mind is as sustainability, environmentally-oriented activities, and more comprehensive reporting become more mainstream it is increasingly important for management to focus on which pieces of data are applicable to specific organizations. Reporting and analyzing a wide variety of information is, or course, a worthy goal and may indeed add value to the organization, but the data reported must be relevant to end users. Assembling a report, or including data simply for the sake of including additional information will not, by itself, increase the value delivered to the market by an organization.

Flexible Purpose Corporations

Benefit corporations, despite the upsides and increased transparency associated with them, may institute and impose restrictions and guidelines that may not be applicable to every organization or industry group. At the core of the idea, benefit corporations represent an alternative structure that may offer more flexibility and optionality for organizations seeking to adopt and implement a more comprehensive reporting structure. Drilling down to the implementation and continued adoption of an integrated reporting structure, a flexible purpose structure enables management and directors to embed nonfinancial information and data into how these flows of data are communicated. Flexible purpose corporations may even enable organizations that may not qualify or fit within traditional sustainability conversations to begin the process of incorporating more types of information into the reporting process. With this connection, bridging the gap between the current market participants, sustainability reporting, and the ability to communicate different types of data to different stakeholders, represents a method by which management professionals can improve both the flow of data and performance of the organization.

For example, establishing a flexible purpose corporation, or even just including certain language related to a more flexible and dynamic corporate structure can enable management to plan and invest not only for the short term but for the longer term as well. Specifically, reflecting the reality that many organizations and management professionals tasked with leading these firms face tremendous pressure to meet and exceed financial targets, a flexible purpose corporation may provide the needed flexibility to begin the conversation around including, and managing for, financial and nonfinancial goals and metrics. Integrating different parts and aspects of how the organization operates, reports information, and communicates these results to stakeholders is a logical step, but in addition to management commitment, these initiatives must also be accompanied by a comprehensive and systemic change in how data are reported. Taking a look at some of the items to help begin this discussion, and keeping mind that these steps are a step toward the eventual full integration and implementation of an integrated report, the following tactics can be used:

1. Identify and analyze stakeholder interest in nonfinancial information. Understanding what specific stakeholders are interested in, how these different stakeholder groups prefer to receive information, and how often these data should ideally be communicated is an important first step in taking any action toward a more comprehensive method of reporting;

2. Analyze which pieces of nonfinancial data are most important for organizational success and growth. Clearly, there are numerous different types of information and data that may be of interest to stakeholder groups, but identifying which classes of information are connected to business performance is a role management should take seriously and dedicate time to addressing;

3. Connect nonfinancial information to the financial performance and success of the organization. While this may seem like a straightforward and logical step, this is often a piece of the analysis that may be overlooked or outsourced to different stakeholder groups. While it may be tempting to take this approach, the reality is that, despite the efforts of other employees, management and other senior leadership must be proactive in these efforts to ensure they are adopted and sustained over time;

4. Roll out integrated reporting on a trial or pilot basis prior to attempting full implementation across the organization or different divisions. Like any other projects or complex initiatives there will inevitably be obstacles, stumbling blocks, and challenges that must be addressed in order to fully recognize the benefits of integrated reporting for an organization. Much like a new product or market is usually introduced on a pilot basis or on an exploratory basis, a new reporting and communication framework should mirror these tactics; and

5. Use business tactics, strategies, and metrics to track the implementation of integrated reporting and to monitor and track progress over time on the effects of reporting changes on the bottom line and operational efficiency. Metrics and key performance indicators (KPIs) drive organizational and operational evaluation and reporting across industry and geographic lines, so the question

is why shouldn't the same tactics be used to monitor a management philosophy or reporting framework? Since the entire idea behind integrated reporting is it will help improve organizational performance, it is logical to then track and monitor the implementation via metrics and KPIs.

Leading Organizations

It is one thing to focus on the potential applications and end results of adopting integrated financial reporting, but it is also important to highlight and examine the results already being achieved by organizations that have already adopted integrated reporting. Taking into account the obvious differences between specific organizations and industries, it is encouraging to see that integrated reporting has been adopted and rolled out by a number of firms across industry and geographic lines. Even more encouragingly, on top of the widespread adoption of integrated reporting evidenced by data available via the IIRC, other organizations are continuing to emphasize nonfinancial and sustainability information. This is an important point to emphasize as management teams grapple with a rapidly evolving business environment that is, on a good day challenging, and mercurial on a routine basis. Put another way, integrated reporting need not be implemented as an all-or-nothing initiative, but instead can build on and improve existing reporting frameworks, policies, and concepts.

As with any innovative idea or concept, there will inevitably be some organizations playing a leadership role in this area versus organizations just beginning this internal discussion. One fact about the current status of integrated reporting apparently producing broad-based support is the variety of organizations that have successfully adopted this framework. Linking back to the earlier point about the importance of multiple industry support, this framework has been implemented by a large number of organizations, which also serve as leaders in respective field. Representing organizations with global operations, and active in different industries, the brief overviews and analyses of these companies provide actionable insights for management professionals seeking to benchmark and mirror best practices.

It is important to recognize that while many of the leading organizations using integrated reporting are among the largest organizations on a global basis, the trend and path of future implementation will inevitably move toward smaller organizations and result in a more widespread adoption and implementation of this tool across industry lines. It is also worth noting that the subset of organizations selected here for inclusion in this research only represent a small sample of the organizations that have adopted integrated reporting. Additionally, these organizations span industry lines, geographic boundaries, and have experimented to different extents with the adoption of other types of nonfinancial reporting frameworks.

There are hundreds of organizations and management teams that have adopted an integrated reporting framework, and an analysis of those organizations alone would provide enough material for an entire book. Rather, the aim of this selection was to highlight two distinct pieces of information. First, the organizations were selected to provide a sample of industries influenced by integrated reporting, and the broader inclusion of nonfinancial information into reporting frameworks. This fact, driven by a confluence of forces both internal and external to the specific organization is a reality professionals must face across industry and geographic lines. Second, and importantly as it is associated with the coveted label of thought leadership, is the fact that not every organization that implements integrated reporting has been traditionally classified as an environmentally oriented organization. In fact, some of the entities chosen for analysis in this book operate in extractive and capital intensive areas that have, all too often in the past, contributed to negative economic externalities and other harmful factors.

The adoption of integrated reporting demonstrates that even if an organization or business model has not been constructed or run as an environmentally aware organization in the past, it does not mean integrated reporting is not an applicable tool. Last, the subset of organizations selected for analysis, which admittedly is a very small percentage of total reporting firms, was put together to reflect a diverse geographical analysis, with every major market represented by at least one organization. Taking this broad lens of analysis is important in an environment that is global, interconnected, and increasingly influenced by forces from nondomestic markets. Also, and this point cannot be overlooked, global supply chains span the world, engage thousands of suppliers and other partner organizations, and must contend with a variety of legal, cultural, and societal expectations.

Taking these forces into account, the following organizations (in a number of different industries, serving different customer segments, and answerable to a variety of regulators) were selected, again taking into account geographic and industrial diversity and duration of integrated reporting.

Note: All information referenced on these leading organizations was gathered from publicly available sources, usually organizational websites and publications.

Apple, Inc.

No analysis of the modern business landscape would be complete without at least a mention of Apple, Inc. and the impact this organization has on how business is conducted both within the United States and on an international basis. The reach and influence of the products introduced by Apple into the marketplace is difficult to overstate, including the iPhone, iPad, and the initial combination of iPod and iTunes, which revolutionized the music industry and landscape when first introduced. Much has been written about the financial prowess and success of the organization from both a revenue and profitability perspective, as well from a production perspective, considering the sheer number of units produced and sold by Apple on a continuous basis. While it is clear that Apple has achieved dramatic and market leading profitability and growth versus the competition, including the global competitor Samsung, there remains an aspect of performance that has not been as completely analyzed to date. Sustainability, as it pertains to both supply chain operations and the manner in which the organization is powered and driven, represents a major source of interest and concern for senior management. The implications, as they relate to the global supply chain of Apple are worthy of analysis and examination in and of themselves. This commitment to sustainability has been actualized by various initiatives and projects alongside investments in product development. Specifically, sustainability initiatives and projects connected to supply chain issues include the following progress and results in the 2017 sustainability progress report:

- The carbon footprint of the organization shrank by 23% from 2015 to 2016, declining from 38.4 million metric tons to 29.5 million metric tons.
- By the end of 2016 Apple had conducted 34 energy audits at supplier facilities, which identified over $55 million in annual savings opportunities, with an average payback period of about 1.4 years.
- The energy improvements in 2016 alone avoided more than 150,000 metric tons of carbon dioxide.

The sustainability efforts and initiatives underway at Apple, as they pertain to their supply chain partners including the sample of projects outlined above are impressive in their own right, but are connected to other efforts underway at Apple corporate headquarters that are powering the organization. Manufacturing, shipping, and operating the various products and services offered by the firm to the marketplace clearly consume massive amounts of energy, but there is also the matter of how the offices and organization itself are powered. Factoring this aspect and segment of operations into the management and growth of the organization, the senior management of the firm has embraced the concept of renewable energy in a major way. This is centered around the construction of new corporate headquarters in Cupertino, which will be the largest LEED Platinum-certified office building in North America. In addition to the facility itself, which is built with sustainable technology a primary facet of construction, there are also onsite facilities dedicated to energy intensive research and development that must be powered.

Satisfying these power requirements and demands is where the innovation and creativity truly is on display along with the commitment of senior management toward using renewable energy to power operations. Focusing specifically on the integration of renewable and clean power options into the core of the organization, Apple has made a definitive shift toward renewable energy throughout its front line and back office operations. Statistics supporting this organizational belief is that nearly 100% of supply chain and corporate operations are now powered by renewable energy sources. In addition to using energy provided by external third parties, the organization currently has 15 renewable energy sites currently in operation and an additional 10 sites are under construction.

Apple does not issue a single integrated financial report and has not, to date, provided market indications that this is the ultimate end goal, but it is interesting to make note of how such a large consumer technology organization has embraced sustainability. Issuing a comprehensive integrated report is, of course, a complex and multifaceted undertaking and one that the senior management at Apple surely would consider at some point. Regardless of the ultimate outcome, however, the implications that can, and should be, extracted from the enthusiasm related to sustainability actions undertaken by Apple are profound. First, the fact that a market-leading organization, which manages to successfully blend technological innovation and consumer satisfaction, is also adopting sustainability initiatives is a signal of the paradigm shift currently underway in the market. Second, the connection and linkage between the core operations of a business, namely energy intensive research and development actions, and renewable energy projects developed to help fuel these actions represents a definitive business case other organizations could possible emulate. Third, and arguably the most important insight that can be gleaned from these initiatives, is the reality that organizations can implement these different ideas and projects in ways offering value to both the specific business and the broader marketplace environment.

Eni: Italian Oil Organization

Eni is one of the largest oil and natural gas organizations in the world; it is headquartered in Western Europe (Italy) but operates on a global scale. Continuing analysis of this organization was a deliberate choice and highlights the connection of integrated reporting with prior initiatives but also differentiates the intersection of financial and operational data from previous sustainability reporting frameworks. Framed in the context of sustainability, including an oil and natural gas organization may not seem to make sense, but this is where integrated reporting is distinct from previous initiatives. In addition to including data on the current state of operations, the management team is also able to communicate the status of future-oriented projects to create and present a comprehensive picture of organizational performance. These statistics included below illustrate the concept of the multiple capital model and integrated reporting at large, as it is put into place at Eni.

The ability of management to craft, evaluate, and report future-oriented projects is critically important in the oil and natural gas industry, where financial and operational performance can be dramatically impacted by external forces and shocks. In addition to the commodity pressure and swings that routinely influence this industry, the continued price pressure on oil requires management to be more creative moving forward. As if these forces were not enough to contend with, the interest and demand for renewable energy sources by consumers, stakeholders, and regulators continues to increase. This convergence of traditional industry forces, changing consumer tastes, environmental regulations, and the financial implications of the above represent a fundamental challenge to how Eni management should evaluate decisions moving forward.

Drilling down into the specific content of the Eni annual report, the organization and management exert a significant amount of effort to not only illustrate the nonfinancial metrics important to the organization, but also to connect nonfinancial information to the bottom line results currently achieved by the organization. Breaking down these different categories of information, and establishing KPIs to track and measure operational and financial performance are important step toward not only reporting the business in a comprehensive manner, but also managing the business in such a manner. This once again illustrates the importance of connecting the reporting of different types of information to how the organization tracks financial performance. In the case of Eni, several general categories of information are most likely to be put into place and communicated to different stakeholder groups.

Included in the business model category and section of the annual integrated report is the importance that the business is conducted in both an operational manner, a financial manner, and in a manner taking into account the sustainability analysis. Breaking down these different areas, and taking into account the importance of nonfinancial information for the long-term success of any organization is an embedded and critical part of any integrated report and reporting process. In addition to reporting this information, included in both operational reports and the annual integrated report, the organization also breaks down the reporting, benefits, and value proposition for stakeholders. Differentiating the KPIs, the value creation for the organization, and the value creation for Eni's stakeholders allows management to not only highlight information reported by the organization, but how this information is communicated and reported to stakeholders.

Breaking it down in an integrated reporting client, the following categories are clearly labeled and differentiated to help with the understanding of information:

1. Operating performance, both related to the financial valuation, increases via the increasing value of certain assets and reserves, enlarging the portfolio of renewable and nonrenewable resources, and the reduction of emissions linked to energy production. Financial performance, from a short-term perspective and longer-term efficiency gains, while attracting the majority of attention and focus, is merely the end result of operational performance and is not a substitute.
2. Environmental performance, which is an extremely relevant and timely issue for an organization in the oil, natural gas, and other extractive industries, also pertains to how the organization is investing in energy efficiency initiatives. Breaking down the reserves by type, and acknowledging the reduction and

evaluation of emissions, including hydrocarbons and renewable energy. Drilling down, and connecting the strategy and strategic decision-making to the reporting of information is required, including water utilization, energy efficiency, and developing green energy and products to augment existing portfolios.

3. Innovation and research is a core competency related toward technology and intellectual property across industry lines, but is especially important for an industry strongly influenced by regulations and other forces. Developing new technologies and tools to improve the efficiency and productivity of assets and platforms, and developing new licenses, partnerships, and opportunities to collaborate across industry lines are both examples of innovation, and drive operations forward. In addition to linking activities and operations, this integrated report also provides users with an opportunity to evaluate and judge the success of the organization's strategic plan.

One of the core aspects of an integrated reporting framework is the fact that, in addition to documenting the performance of the organization during the current period, the strategic planning process is also highlighted. This is especially important in the energy production and distribution industry where energy prices, increased scrutiny from regulators and stakeholders, and the increased interest in renewable energy create an increasingly competitive environment. Management professionals must be able to document and explain the strategic decision-making process. Breaking these factors down, Eni, which is recognized as an early adopter and innovator in the field of integrated reporting, analyzes the various risk factors that may influence the organization moving forward. Particularly as the organization continues to face commodity and price pressures throughout the entire production and distribution process. Finding efficiencies, planning for the medium and long term, and incorporating various external risks appear to only become more important as the company moves forward.

Novo Nordisk: Pharmaceutical Organization

Novo Nordisk, a Scandinavian pharmaceutical organization, is often held up as an almost ideal representation of an organization that has effectively managed to integrate financial and nonfinancial metrics into how it is managed and evaluated. A component of both the personal belief and ethos of the management team, and perhaps a reflection of the methodology of government presence in the area, Novo Nordisk has long emphasized the importance of sustainable growth in an environmentally conscious manner. Such an approach, in addition to differentiating the organization from other competitors in the landscape, has not had a negative impact on the financial performance of the organization during the medium or long term.

Novo Nordisk has issued a comprehensive integrated report, including and analyzing performance linked to operational, financial, and environmental issues since 2004. Available directly on the organizational homepage, a statement is made that issuing an integrated report enables a more accurate and comprehensive evaluation of how the firm is performing. Leading off the report is a statement from the CEO emphasizing the importance of sustainable growth to the organization, including a documentation of initiatives and efforts underway to achieve growth sustainable over the medium and long term. Embedded in the reporting and operating performance of the organization is the triple bottom line principle, anchored and emphasized in the company's articles of association. Building on this inclusion, the organization also includes a specific reference to what exactly sustainability means in terms of how the organization operates and performs linking together financial, social, and environmental operations of the firm.

Reporting on these different areas not only reinforces the commitment of the organization to operate in a socially and environmentally responsible manner, but also provides an opportunity for management to establish benchmarks. Some of the statistics reported in the report include the following:

- 79% of the power (electricity) used by the organization is generated by renewable sources of energy, and are forecasted to save millions of gallons of water by 2018.
- By 2020, the organization plans and is working toward generating all power used in operations from renewable sources.
- In an effort to reduce CO_2 emissions in alignment with other longer-term organizational objectives, management at the organization is encouraging employees to utilize virtual meetings, increasing the utilization of virtual meetings by 25% over the last several years.

Even in light of these long-term investments, working toward environmental and sustainability goals, including a socially conscious component, the financial performance of the organization has not suffered. Net sales, denominated in DKK, increased by over 30% during the time period between 2013–2017, demonstrating robust financial growth and performance even in light of increasing pressure from global competition and increased competition from generics.

Clearly the management team at Novo Nordisk has created, and continues to sustain, a company culture and environment conducive to managing the business for the medium and long term; however, the strongest culture will not offset negative financial effects or if the organization fails to achieve stated objectives. The impressive financial growth and performance in a global industry that over the same time period has gone through a period of consolidation, increased pressure from generics, and price pressure from emerging competition is especially impressive. Acknowledging the reality that the pharmaceutical industry is both incredibly competitive and constrained by a number of legal guidelines and parameters, it can be a challenge to find and develop organic growth opportunities. Novo Nordisk, seeming to buck the larger industry trend toward consolidation and short termism, has found a method to focus on financial performance in a sustainable manner.

Eisai

Eisai, also in the pharmaceutical industry, is also an example of an organization that has, despite financial and competitive pressures, embraced a long-term view of not only how the organization should perform but how the organization should interact with the broader stakeholder environment. Perhaps a partial reflection of societal norms in place guiding how businesses should treat and interact with different stakeholder groups, Eisai is one of over 300 organizations listed and traded in Japan that have implemented integrated reporting. This concentration of organizations utilizing an integrated reporting framework provides a unique opportunity to not only examine the financial impact of using this framework, but also an occasion to examine what other external forces may have influenced their decision.

Leveraging internal expertise embedded within the organization, specifically the ability to produce and distribute pharmaceuticals across numerous geographic boundaries, Eisai launched several initiatives that appear to embrace a stakeholder-oriented model of management and behavior. Specifically, distributing and providing low to no-cost vaccines across the African continent illustrates the commitment of management to operating in a globally aware and stakeholder-oriented manner. It is important to note that, regardless of the specific industry that is the focus in any current analysis, the broader business landscape and corporate environment appears to drive the adoption of sustainability performance. Whether it is due to the inclusion of employee and governmental stakeholder groups at the board level, or the reality that macroeconomic trends have negatively impacted growth overall, a strict evaluation of financial performance may not be as appropriate as in other markets. Adopting an integrated reporting framework, and including a multiple capital model as a part of this reporting framework, allows management professionals to focus on developing and communicating a comprehensive view of organizational performance.

Taking a closer look at the most current integrated report (2017) issued by the organization, and beginning with the first page of the report, the six capitals and connections to value creation at an organizational level are clear. In addition to highlighting and explaining the different types of capital, Eisai also expands upon this definition be layering four different perspectives, connected to the balanced scorecard. More importantly, and arguably more important than simply listing what the six capitals mean to the organization is the inclusion of goals, objectives, and business connections of these ideas to how Eisai runs and operates the business. Specifically, and illustrated at the very beginning of the integrated report, Eisai management sets targets, business activities, and results to bridge the gap between conceptual and business application. Serving as a potential for other organizations to replicate also illustrates the potential of integrated reporting to add value and deliver results across different industry lines.

Deliberately addressing the key shortcomings of prior initiatives connected to reporting nonfinancial and sustainability information, the management at Eisai has also highlighted the importance of establishing and reporting information that is material to the decision-making process. Outlined in a three step process, documented below, the organization establishes and communicates how different types of information are analyzed, quantified, and reported to stakeholders. The process includes the following steps to facilitate the reporting of information:

1. Identification of the issues, meaning that the organization works with both internal and external resources to identify and highlight what types of information should be included and reported;
2. Prioritization of the information, meaning that even after identifying the types and classes of information that are material to the business, not every piece of information is equally as important to the market; and
3. Review, revise, and update, which is particularly important in the field of nonfinancial and sustainability information. Especially with the wide array of options out there for organizations to reference and use, keeping abreast of changes in the market is especially important for organizations seeking to remain relevant.

Establishing these criteria and ground rules, however, is just the first step in quantifying and reporting different classes of information. Building upon these introductory classifications and different types of information, and a critical part of communicating the benefits of integrated reporting this information to stakeholders, Eisai also embeds pieces of its corporate philosophy in the articles of incorporation. Integrating the core values and ideas of integrated reporting, nonfinancial information, and a more a comprehensive set of metrics to evaluate and judge organizational performance is an important step in the development and advancement of integrated reporting on a more broad-based level.

American Electric Power (AEP)

American Electric Power was selected for inclusion in this analysis for the reasons that it has been issuing an integrated financial reporting framework since 2012, and that the management team has chosen to do so in an industry sector not necessarily associated with environmentally sustainable operations. It is true that AEP operates a number of coal-fired power plants, which would not fit into a sustainability framework or ethos, but that does not tell the entire story of the organization nor the future direction management intends to travel. Specifically, by focusing on both current financial performance and longer-term strategic growth, management must not only plan for the next quarter, but for the next multiyear period. It is important to acknowledge, and certainly a reality for any organization seeking to implement an integrated report, that politics and governmental policies do influence the business decision-making process.

Investing for the long term, especially in a business environment and industry so driven and guided by regulation, external forces and stakeholder pressure can be extraordinarily difficult to adjust to. Particularly if senior management must engage and report quarterly financial performance and results to analysts, and if the organization has not achieved benchmark results the pressure to emphasize short-term performance can be tremendous. It is realistically possible even in favorable business environments with an engaged stakeholder group and positive operational forces that an organization will stumble from time to time on a financial basis. Taking these facts into account, and comparing them to situations and variables facing energy and other extractive oriented organizations and industries, which are not always favorable or positive in nature, the potential for short term financial missteps only increase, which will inevitably place pressure on management to act in the interest of short term shareholders versus a more holistic type of organizational return. In that context it is even more important for management professionals to be proactive, engage with external stakeholders, and report information on a comprehensive basis.

Looking into the specific actions undertaken by AEP management, it is also important to recognize that the utility business in the United States, previously highly regulated and predictable in nature, has transitioned to an industry that is still regulated, although in the midst of disruption. Many of these same forces, namely sustainability and an increased interest by stakeholders in how an organization generates returns, are influencing organizations such as AEP. To be sure, coal-fired power plants are still in operation with new iterations both in the pipeline and coming to market, but that is just one aspect of the business. Nuclear power, while containing operational risks of its own, is a source of power that is being looked into as a viable alternative. Some market commentators have doubts as to the legitimacy of initiatives by organizations such as AEP and other actors in similar industry spaces, so the importance of quantifying these efforts is critical. This quantification of data, in addition to being good business, also directly connects to the value generated by an integrated reporting framework. Some examples of how these efforts are quantified, taken directly from the AEP website, include the following:

- $8.7 billion in estimated total investments in environmental controls between 2000 and 2017 to reduce emissions
- 33% reduction in water withdrawal in 2016 compared to 2014
- 4166 MW in total renewable portfolio projects
- 56% reduction in CO_2 emissions from 2000 to 2017
- 94% reduction in SO_2 emissions from 2000 to 2017

These achievements are significant in their own right, but only represent a partial perspective of the efforts underway at AEP. Stakeholder engagement is an idea and concept represented prominently on the AEP home page, with multiple goals included in why engagement is imperative. Said efforts and rationale include, but are not limited to addressing environmental, social, and governance (ESG) issues for investors, are influencing the narrative around organizational direction, may spur certain types of activism, and may support the long-term strategy of the organization. These and other goals of this stakeholder strategy appear to mirror closely some of the underlying drivers and goals of integrated reporting itself. It should come as no surprise then that AEP has been issuing an integrated report since 2012 and had been publishing an array of sustainability information prior to that. It is also evident that, while making investments and undertaking actions for the future are popular with stakeholder groups, the financial ramifications of these actions must also be taken into account.

The management of AEP, even in a volatile business environment that has seen changes in how several significant projects are performing, has generated several notable financial successes. Financial metrics, publicly available via the AEP annual report include the following during the period 2012–2016:

- An increase in revenue from $14.2 billion USD to $16.3 billion USD
- Increase in common equity from $15.2 billion USD to $17.3 billion USD
- Book value per share increasing from $31.35 per share to $35.38 per share
- Cash dividends per share increasing from $1.88 per share to $2.27 per share

These increases in revenue and other financial metrics alongside increases and improvements in environmental performance highlight the benefits of making strides to improve the organization in a manner cognizant of both financial and nonfinancial forces. Regardless of individual opinion or market commentary on the rate-regulated utility industry, the fact remains that while simultaneously taking steps to reduce environmental externalities, the organization has also achieved successful financial performance.

Southwest

Southwest is interesting for an organization operating in an industry usually categorized by competitiveness, continuously striving for fuel efficiency, and customer service that can vary wildly. It is also well known for issuing a comprehensive integrated report ranking among the most highly recognized reports among North American firms. This reporting framework and structure, in addition to being an indication of the mindset and perspective of management with regards to sustainable growth, also represent the ethos of management echoed throughout the organization. Specifically, Southwest is also known for employee training, development, and creating a work environment hospitable for both employees and customers travelling with the organization. While these initiatives do result in higher levels of costs in certain areas versus competitors, it has not harmed or had a detrimental financial impact on the organization. In fact, compared to peers and as an especially interesting case in the financially competitive U.S. airline market, Southwest has generated superior financial returns, even during the economic downturn of 2007–2009.

Even in the highly competitive global airline business, it is possible for organizations to not only invest in financial performance, but to also implement strategies and tactics to develop a broad base of performance over longer periods of time. Southwest, because of the nature of its activity, does indeed generate significant pollutants and CO_2 emissions. Building up a global airline network requires and generates some level of energy consumption and pollution. That said, just because an organization operates in an industry with a history of pollution and energy intensive operations does not automatically make the adoption of environmentally sensitive and oriented policies a challenge. Rather, as perceived by Southwest, it is an opportunity, which is evident both in qualitative and quantitative information and characteristics. Qualitative information and data, including but not limited to employee and customer service metrics and information represent important information for stakeholders, but must be supported and framed by quantitative data. Bifurcating the types of quantitative information generated and published by an organization, while not sacrificing either transparency or quality of end-user data, both operational and financial information must be included and communicated out to external stakeholders. Every organization and every industry are different, but there are several trends, including connecting operational performance to bottom-line performance, which apply across industry lines.

Specifically, several positive statistics and trends related to energy consumption and pollution are as follows:

- Between 2005 and 2016 Southwest has achieved a 30.6% improvement in jet fuel efficiency, which not only reduces pollutants and a CO_2 footprint, but also lowers the costs associated with this input cost.
- Starting in 2013, the management team at Southwest began a corporate sponsored recycling program, and in one case was able to reduce the total amount sent to landfills by 5500 pounds simply by repurposing life jackets instead of discarding them.
- Working in conjunction with the Salvation Army, items left on airplanes and never subsequently claimed are sold via a national distributor with the proceeds donated to charity, enhancing the connection between the organization and the broader community.

In the case of Southwest, drilling in and connecting the operations of the business to various sustainability and other nonfinancial information, in this case lower emissions, reduced fuel costs, and less expenses for waste disposal, to the core of the business is relatively straightforward. In addition to the environmental savings and benefits of improving the sustainability of business operations, these savings also provide management with the ability to expand and grow the business. Traditionally known as a regional player in the airline landscape, Southwest now services the 48 contiguous states from 13 gateway airports, and as is launching an international expansion for the first time in its corporate history. While it is clear that some of these expansion efforts are driven by competitive forces, these investments, in both sustainability and environmental efforts as well as service expansion, have resulted in strong financial performance.

This is an important point to emphasize in the conversation and dialogue around integrated reporting; even as integrated reporting is implemented, including financial investments into the business, financial performance need not be sacrificed. Between 2012 and 2016, and resulting in $2.2 billion of income in 2016, the income generated by the organization has increased by 433% even as the global airline business continues to increase in competitiveness. Especially in a highly competitive and regulated business industry such as the global airline business, this profit growth is impressive considering the increase in global competition, which has caused much managerial angst. Put simply, and highlighted by the impressive performance of Southwest, the connection between integrated reporting, nonfinancial data and information, and financial performance is clear.

Coca-Cola

Although Coca-Cola has yet to issue a formal integrated report as per the integrated reporting framework, the information communicated by this organization to the external environment is interesting for several reasons. First, the company produces and communicates sustainability and water-related information in a manner aligned with other data produced and disseminated by the organization. Connecting these two different items is important because it creates a beneficial cycle where operational and sustainability data can, as it should, influence the financially oriented decisions underway in the organization. Coca-Cola is an interesting case study and example of an organization adopting integrated financial reporting because, as is often the case, the end result and reports did not occur overnight (Figure 4.1).

The perception of certain types of organizations and industries with a large environmental impact, such as mining, timber, or other extractive industries is well known, but it is also important to acknowledge the environmental impact of food service organizations. Connecting to the broader discussion around the water stewardship initiatives underway at the organization, it becomes readily apparent that the journey toward integrated reporting can begin at an organization in any market and evolve over time. Beginning with the sustainable aspect of operations, as it connects to water recycling and water utilization, is a logical place for a water-intensive firm such as Coca-Cola to begin nonfinancial analysis, but every organization will have an appropriate place to begin with their nonfinancial reporting and communication. Water stewardship, quantifying the impact of water

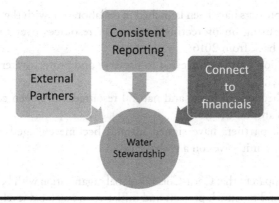

Figure 4.1   Sustainability at Coca-Cola.

recycling and utilization, and connecting the efforts and initiatives connected to nonfinancial reporting provide management with an appropriate platform to communicate these findings to external stakeholders.

Every organization has certain classes and types of information and data that are particularly important for the management and interpretation of financial results over the medium and long term. Clearly, the specifics of implementation and reporting of nonstandardized information will take a certain amount of time, investments, and involve the training of employees. In addition, it is also important to quantify the effect of nonfinancial information on organizational results from a financial perspective. Drilling down through some of the publicly available information on the investments and results of these sustainability linked initiatives, several key statistics and pieces of information appear particularly relevant. As of 2016, the information linked to sustainability, specifically water stewardship and recycling projects include the following:

■ Coca-Cola is giving back, through organizational initiatives, 115% of the water used in products to communities and surrounding areas.
■ The core pillars of water stewardship and the reporting of this information center around (1) providing safe access to water resources, (2) restoring and protecting existing resources, and (3) being a proponent for productive and sustainable uses of water resources.

In addition to these goals, which while impressive are strictly qualitative in nature, the organization is also measuring and tracking both the investments in these areas and the results generated:

■ 248 water partnership and stewardship projects in 2000 communities across 71 countries;

- Over 50 projects have been launched in collaboration with the World Wildlife Fund, focusing on protecting fresh water resources over the last 9 years, counting back from 2016;
- $300 million has been invested to preserve and protect water resources on a global level;
- 187,000 hectares of forest and natural resources have been conserved in 20 countries around the world;
- Over 400 partners have signed up and become engaged with the water stewardship initiatives on a global level.

While it is apparent that Coca-Cola is a global organization with both the financial and human capital to launch projects and initiatives on a global level, the model and methodology put into place at Coca-Cola can, and should be, replicated by other organizations in the water and water service areas. Seeking to improve efficiency and reduce operational costs is something every management team should strive to achieve on a continuous basis. Every business, large or small, has to work with stakeholders, partners, and other organizations to coordinate initiatives and projects.

Clorox

Clorox represents perhaps the most interesting implementation story of an organization that has put an integrated reporting framework into place, considering the fact that it is a consumer product company operating across a range of product lines. Specifically, the cleaning and industrial products that form the core of the business lines produced by Clorox may, if not disposed of properly, contribute directly to environmental degradation and harm; this potential connection makes sustainability initiatives all the more important. Also worthy of note is while there is a business-to-business component of Clorox's business model, a large percentage of business operations are linked to the consumer-facing side of the organization. Consumers, who account for 70% of GDP in the United States and drive a substantial amount of economic activity and growth on a global basis, are increasingly applying pressure as to how management professionals act and engage with stakeholders.

Consumers, especially in industrialized and service marketplaces, seem to be showing an increased interest and concern over just how organizations produce products, deliver services, and generate financial performance over the medium and longer term. Navigating the sometimes mercurial consumer landscape, including the shifting nature of tastes, preferences, and requirements means that management must be adaptable and flexible in how to achieve these goals. Sustainability, especially for a consumer-oriented and focused company such as Clorox, is a fact that must be integrated into both current and forward-looking operations. Specifically, and highlighted throughout the 2017 integrated report, the following facts and progress illustrate the focus and attention paid by management on these issues:

1. By 2017, Clorox has made sustainability improvements to 34% of the total product portfolio, with a publicized goal of 50% by 2020.
2. Since 2011, the organization has reduced greenhouse gas emissions by 18%, water usage by 21%, energy usage by 15%, and waste materials delivered to landfills by 41%.

Putting financial resources behind verbal commitments to invest in local and community-based activities, the organization invested over $11 million USD in cash grants, product donations, and cause marketing activities.

Circling back to the broader base of support for sustainable and environmentally conscious activities and investments by organizations and individuals, Clorox is also a signatory to the United Nations Global Compact. Such a framework, in this case the UNGC, delivers two messages to the marketplace. First, it signals to all stakeholder groups that Clorox and the management professionals leading the organization are committed to sustainable activities and environmentally oriented actions. Such communication also allows management to accurately frame the strategic decision-making process within the context of financial and operational investments. Second, it communicates to shareholders in the financial community the reality that Clorox may, from time to time, subordinate short-term financial performance and metrics to build for the future, develop a more sustainable business model, and deliver growth over a continuum of time periods. Last, reinforcing the reality that the organization is placing a definitive amount of emphasis on these matters, are the other external certifications and recognition the organization has received. These include, but are not limited to being recognized by the U.S. Environmental Protection Association as a Safer Choice Partner of the Year in 2017, and being named to the top 100 companies on the Best Corporate Citizens list by Corporate Responsibility magazine.

With all of these sustainability and long-term investments and plans, however, a common question is do these activities come at the expense of financial performance and satisfaction of financial shareholders? Additionally, and of importance to shareholders and stakeholders involved with the organization, the most recent financial results are:

■ An increase of 4% of sales, with increases registered on a quarter to quarter basis.
■ 9% increase in diluted EPS in 2017, following an 8% increase in 2016.
■ A 13% increase in cash from continuing operations from 2016 to 2017, resulting in a positive cash flow from operations totaling $871 USD (in millions).

Regardless of whether Clorox, and the management team tasked with leading the organization forward are evaluated from a strictly financial perspective or from a more comprehensive perspective, there are indications of successful management from virtually every angle. Taking into account the competitive environment, including but not limited to the consumer-oriented approach management professionals must take to succeed in the current environment, the success and performance of the organization is all the more impressive. Framed in this context, both the operational and financial success of the organization can, and often are, used as benchmarks and guidelines for other entities to emulate and strive to obtain.

JLL

A cursory review and examination of integrated reporting, and the applications of this framework may lead reviewers and users to estimate and postulate it is an idea meant for industrial organizations. Categorizing, analyzing, and reporting different classes of information and data may indeed seem to make most sense for organizations and industries that not only operate in an array of geographic areas, but who also have to contend with organizations that produce many different streams of operational information. That said, it is important to recognize and realize that service organizations, including professional service organizations operating on a standalone basis and organizations that service industrial firms may also qualify for integrated reporting implementation. In fact, taking into account stakeholder pressures that can emerge from both financial and nonfinancial arenas, it can be argued that operational pressures and force may be even more pronounced for service organizations than for other types of organizations. Specifically, and acknowledging the reality that a firm such as JLL is one of many organizations employing a highly educated and increasingly socially conscious workforce, the following is something that should be, and increasingly is, acknowledged.

Instead of being a stakeholder-driven initiative, or an idea created and communicated by external stakeholder groups, increasingly employees will represent a driving force for the adoption of a more comprehensive reporting framework. Taking this fact into account is important for at least two of the following reasons, both of which are applicable for service and industrially oriented organizations. First, employee engagement, development, and creating a talent pipeline to sustain a dynamic business environment is effective management and a component of the integrated reporting framework. Specifically, engagement with employees and other internal stakeholder groups is important for a management team developing and sustaining a culture of long-term thinking and execution. Second, connecting directly to the integrated reporting framework and multiple capital model, human and intellectual capital are both core areas of the reporting structure that drives communication and information from the inside to the outside of the organization.

Factoring in this dual force pressure and information from both internal and external forces, it is increasingly clear that integrated reporting and the multiple capital model are indeed applicable for service firms. Unique to JLL but a situation possibly arising for other service and service-oriented organizations is the relationship JLL has with other industries. In the case of JLL, the industry serviced by this organization is the real estate business. Clearly the real estate business and industry will be influenced and impacted by the growing interest in both financial and nonfinancial information. Furthermore, the real estate industry landscape JLL operates in is influenced by both sustainability and the need for more comprehensive information in the following areas:

1. The carbon footprint of individual buildings and developments, which can be broken down into several areas. Specifically, how much electricity is used in the operation of these buildings, is the recycling of water and other inputs a component of building operating systems, and are there renewable projects implemented at the location?
2. How much of the overall environmental impact of the developer or building is caused by the supply chain? Meaning that there is a long line of contractors and sub-contractors tasked with assisting with the completion of the structure and embedded systems. One question to ask is whether or not these contractors and sub-contractors, who play a large role in the finished product, operate in an environmentally sensitive and/or conscious manner.
3. Are the buildings and locations LEED certified? This market-leading certification and ranking is a clear method by which the commitment and results of that commitment can and should be communicated to external users. These users can, and often do, include tenants, partners, other real estate developers, and regulators all of which are interested in the performance of the building and overall commercial portfolio.

Taking an inclusive view of both operational and financial performance, several statistics and pieces of information are important for this analysis. Leading off the analysis, it is important to acknowledge the scope of JLL, its operations, and the potential thought leadership such a market position enables the organization and management team to exercise.

■ The organization employs over 77,000 people, serving clients in over 80 counties from more than 280 distinct corporate offices on a global basis.
■ The investment management arm of the business, focusing on real estate investment, has over $60 billion USD under management, ranking it as one the largest and most diverse real estate investment portfolios in the world.
■ In 2016 alone, JLL completed 38,000 leasing transactions, which encompassed 828 million square feet of space, which is part of a total portfolio of over 4.4 billion square feet on a global basis.
■ JLL achieved 14% revenue growth, to $5.8 billion USD, from the previous year as reported in 2016.

The organization has received numerous awards and other indicators of external recognition such as inclusion in the Dow Jones Sustainability Index for North America, being included as a leading ethical organization by the Ethisphere Institute, and ranking as one of the World's Most Admired Companies by *Fortune* for two consecutive years. Such external recognition may seem like simply additional qualitative information and awards not connected to fundamental business performance, but that would represent an incomplete view of just what these awards and external recognition represent, especially for service organizations.

Adopting a more comprehensive reporting framework, especially in the services industry, can be a challenge to sell both internally and externally. Internal challenges may in many instances result from a number of internal stakeholder groups bringing up the following issues. First, as a services industry, and especially for established firms with a large and varied client base, management may not feel time is well spent by focusing on sustainability and other nonfinancial metrics. This presents a potential loss of revenue and market leadership opportunity as organizations, which assuredly include clients of service firms, move in this direction. As operations and management move toward a more comprehensive view of performance, these firms will increasingly expect advisory services and expertise in these areas. Second, communicating the initiatives and information around this idea to financial and nonfinancial stakeholders is an important step in transitioning the organization to a more forward-looking entity. Put simply, operations drive performance, nevertheless it is important to not only acknowledge this reality but to also ensure shareholders and stakeholders understand just how strong this connection is for performance.

Stakeholders, even those who would otherwise be interested in investing in organizations with sustainable aspirations, goals, and operations, must be presented with sufficient financial incentives for doing so. Even as larger institutional stakeholders and shareholders commit capital and resources to these processes and projects, any transition in how data are communicated must be facilitated by the management professionals employed at the organization. Data, including both qualitative and quantitative information is what ultimately drives the decision-making process both internal and external to the organization, and must be taken into account as service firms transition to more comprehensive reporting structures. The benefits and downsides, including costs and necessary investments necessary to implement such a framework are more obvious than would be initially evident from a service-based organization.

General Electric

It is true that the following two pieces of information should be recognized when conducting an analysis of General Electric in the context of sustainability reporting, and the efforts underway toward a more comprehensive framework for communicating information. First, the organization has suffered significant declines in profitability and price per share valuation during 2016 and 2017, as some of the acquisitions have not generated projected returns. Specifically, acquisitions and deployment of capital into capital intensive and industrial areas have resulted in a decline of returns. Second, and arguably more important for the purposes of this analysis is that GE forayed into the sustainability conversation with extensive existing resources to deploy and allocate toward the selected initiatives. Stated another way, the management team in place had substantial resources and existing product lines to leverage, but the ideas and concepts appear applicable to virtually every organization.

Ecomagination, a headline generating business division opened by GE in 2008, represents an entire business line oriented toward sustainability, energy efficiency, and generating insights from business analytics to improve operations. Taking a step back, and acknowledging that the organization is currently facing turmoil and questions regarding the forward direction of the firm, two points are worthy of acknowledgment. First, the fact that a leading global multinational organization launched this division and made such a public commitment in terms of financial and personnel resources indicates the level to which this conversation has moved to in the mainstream. Second, drilling down to the operational reality of operating such a division is the connection made between analytics, business insights, and achieving operational efficiencies.

Building a bridge and connecting the traditionally qualitative field of sustainability—all too often phrased as a conversation of stakeholder initiative—and data analytics represents a replicable path forward and technique for different organizations. Data are what drives organizational decision-making and this is not a point that can, or should be, overlooked or thought of as optional and only appropriate for larger organizations. Management professionals already have reams of information to assist with the decision-making process; why not take that information to make decisions applicable for the long-term health of the organization? Drilling down into the specific information, all of which is publicly available to external users, there are evident connections between core operations and sustainability initiatives.

Connecting these bridges and linkages between industrial activities (forming the core business and machinations of GE) with sustainability and other environmentally oriented initiatives is critical to implement such programs and to sustain them during volatile market conditions. Especially when current market conditions and forces are driving negative market headlines and share price information, being sure these connections are evident both internally and externally is extremely important. Once again, while GE has not, as of this writing, committed to publishing a comprehensive integrated reporting on an annual basis, existing information and statistics are worthy of additional analysis.

The impressive statistical information and results of Ecomagination include, but are not limited to the following information, data, and reports:

1. According to GE research and market interactions, renewable energy will account for two-thirds of all capacity additions in the electric marketplace;
2. By investing in operational and business process efficiency initiatives, including digital solutions across power, aviation, lighting, and beyond there is the potential to realize savings of $81 billion in fuels, avoiding 823 million metric tons of CO_2, and closing the global carbon cap by 30%;
3. Since the division has launched during the 2005–2006 years, management has created a corporate strategy to deliver clean energy solutions that drive positive economic and environmental outcomes;
4. During the lifespan of Ecomagination the organization has invested a total of $20 billion in cleaner technology solutions, which has generated $270 billion in revenues for the organization;
5. Additionally, greenhouse emissions have been reduced by 42% since 2004;
6. Freshwater used in operations has been cut by 53% since 2006;
7. Management remains committed to investing yet another $5 billion in Ecomagination operations by 2020;
8. Connecting management activities and corporate initiatives to employee actions and engagement also represents an important part of maintaining these programs;
9. The 2016 EcoAwards program recognized employee developed projects that have resulted in 22,700 metric tons of CO_2, 24.9 kWh of electricity, and more than $47 million USD in annual cost savings; and
10. Over the last 7 years, the Ecomagination division has sponsored hackathons, open innovation challenges, and other methods to encourage stakeholder engagement in this process.

General Electric, once an example of leading environmental and sustainability operations, has recently experienced turbulence and uncertainty with financial results, however, environmental and sustainability operations will continue to be important for the continued success of GE. Financial performance and operational information are linked together on an intrinsic basis, especially as the organization transitions, evolves, and shifts toward an industrial first organization versus services and capital-based, which led to financial issues on its own accord, especially during the Financial Crisis of 2007–2008. Connecting these concepts and information toward medium and long-term performance is an imperative of management, and a component of the fiduciary duty embedded in the construct of governance.

Technology Organizations

In the current business landscape dominated by technology giants, digitized information, and a globalized landscaped interconnected in virtually every way, it is important that technology companies are equally advised and interested in using integrated reporting, or some other nonfinancial reporting framework. Although much of the operational results and machinations of technology companies are digital in nature and do not engage in extractive or specific heavy industrial activities, much of the back end operations are driven by nontechnology functions. Although cloud servers, mobile apps, and cloud computing operate virtually without tangible assets or a visible footprint, the underlying factors do indeed have an impact on the physical environment. Server farms, the electrical demands necessary to run and manage these server farms, the infrastructure necessary to communicate information across geographic boundaries via physical cable all have an impact on the environment, nonfinancial information, and how the organization will develop and grow in the medium and long term.

Examples of this transition and evolution of reporting at a number of technology organizations is evident in the efforts underway at Facebook, Google, and Amazon. In addition to constructing and investing in modern headquarters and physical infrastructures fully compliant with environmental regulations, there are several other factors at work in the business landscape around these issues. First, as a result of the increasing energy demands and requirements of these organizations, virtually every large technology organization is investing in renewable energy to manage and power server farms. Additionally, due to the rising integration of technology with business operations there is an increasingly high profile connection between energy consumption and technology solutions.

Commonalities

Although the companies referenced in this "Leading Organizations" section of the book represent a wide variety of industries, geographic regions, and end-user groups—many of which are interrelated in the broader business landscape—they are not as disconnected as would initially appear on the surface. Much like any other business trend, theme, or market moving information, and even though the specifics of industries and markets will inevitably differ from time to time it is important to recognize that common themes do exist. In addition to being an intellectually interesting exercise, these common themes and trends also illustrate the fact that adoption of integrated reporting may not be as unique an initiative as it might appear upon initial review. Clearly, the commonalities and themes identified as components of this book are not meant to be an all-inclusive listing of themes and ideas to be considered, but rather should be thought of as a place to begin the

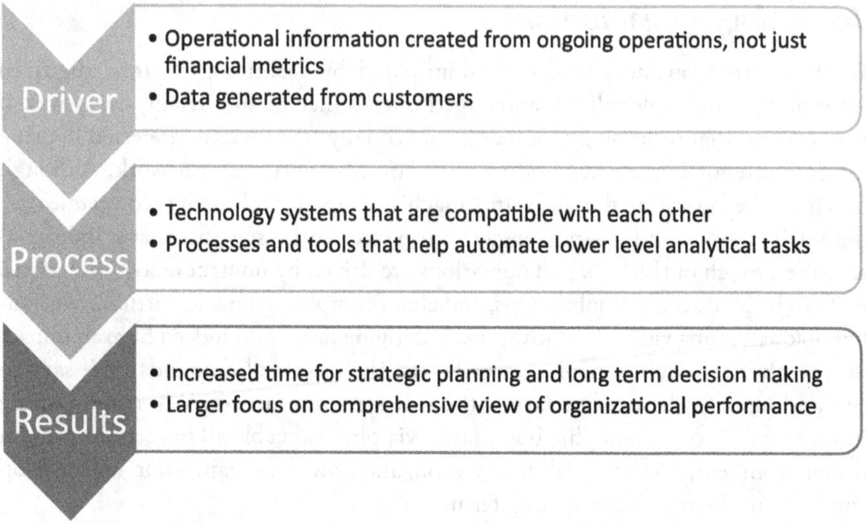

Driver
- Operational information created from ongoing operations, not just financial metrics
- Data generated from customers

Process
- Technology systems that are compatible with each other
- Processes and tools that help automate lower level analytical tasks

Results
- Increased time for strategic planning and long term decision making
- Larger focus on comprehensive view of organizational performance

Figure 4.2   How integrated reporting connects to business objectives.

implementation process. Specifically, the following appear to be worth additional consideration and analysis (Figure 4.2):

1. The underlying business environment of the industry is changing. While this might seem like a throwaway comment or thought, many of the organizations most dramatically impacted by business changes are also most likely to be seeking an idea or platform to help improve performance. Of course, simply realizing the business landscape is changing is insufficient; management teams must be willing and able to enact changes necessary to survive and thrive in a changing market. The fact remains that the business landscape is changing for virtually all organizations, but some industries will experience this disruption at different times than others.

2. Integrated reporting can apply to both consumer-facing organizations and companies involved in business-to-business transactions and industries. At first glance it may seem that consumer-facing organizations such as Clorox or Coca-Cola are more exposed or impacted by the growth of stakeholder interest, as these forces and trends influence a variety of organizations. General Electric, for example, has transitioned from a conglomerate with a presence across the board to an organization primarily focused on providing products and services to industrial clients and partners. Even as this transition was accelerated under recently departed CEO Jeffery Immelt, the importance of sustainability and efficiency has only increased. Framed in this context, the saying that sustainability is good for business appears to be grounded in idealism and business reality.

3. Industry specificity is not as large a consideration for the implementation of integrated reporting as initially might be apparent. Clearly, organizations involved in businesses that use large amounts of natural resources, such as Coca-Cola, may appear to represent early adopters of integrated reporting, but industry specific focus and operations need not limit the adoption of integrated reporting. The differences between what types of information and data are reported in an integrated framework will inevitably vary from firm to firm, but it is important to recognize that there are commonalities that can, and should, be examined to assist in the implementation process.

4. Technology is a part of the integrated reporting process but does not constitute the entirety of the adoption and implementation process, even if the firm in question is a technology-based organization. Artificial intelligence, data automation, blockchain, and the digitization of information across the business landscape continue to change and generate transition themes every organization needs to take into account. Even with the buzz, hype, and increased media coverage pertaining to these topics it is important to realize that technology is not the cure-all for organizational inefficiencies, but merely a platform to generate and analyze different flows of information. Harnessing technology is an important first step and merely represents a first step and tool to help analyze, quantify, and report different flows of information.

5. Successfully engaging with both financial and nonfinancial stakeholders is an important part of the implementation and adoption process of integrated reporting. It is one thing to invest in resources and technology to improve and/ or streamline the reporting process, but stakeholders must be a component of the dialogue to generate effective and robust analyses. Engaging with stakeholders allows management to communicate different types of information to the marketplace in a manner consistent and comparable to other types of information. Issuing consistent types of sources of information is an important part of making nonfinancial information mainstream and part of the dialogue. Making this a continuous part of the reporting and analysis process is a critical step, which ties into an additional point of commonality worthy of consideration.

6. Integrated reporting implementation must, in virtually every case, take place in stages linked to different types of implementation protocols and practices. Sustainability guidelines, operational information, and other nonfinancial information must be incorporated into how the organization discusses and reports information to both internal colleagues and external colleagues. Depending on the organization, certain classes and types of information will be more important for the sustainability conversation, but implementing these into the reporting process will, inevitably, take different periods of time depending on the organization in question.

7. The process will take time, which is an equally important fact to emphasize to internal stakeholders and external users of organizational information.

Contrasting this versus financial machinations that may generate short-term financial beats or superior performance, it is important to emphasize the medium to long-term nature of integrated reporting. While the implementation of integrated reporting may take longer than other organizational initiatives, it is also important to recognize its longer-term benefits. The timeline through which integrated reporting will be implemented at an organization should be a conversation raised by management.

Building from Complementary Work: Other Examples of Nonfinancial Reporting

No reporting framework or any type of idea develops in a vacuum or independently of other actions underway in the marketplace, and this is equally true for integrated reporting as it is for other business initiatives. Integrated reporting, while representing a more comprehensive model of reporting by including a greater variety of information, did not come into existence entirely independently of other trends. Sustainability reporting clearly represents an issue and area of focus discussed by business, academia, and media for decades—this work continues in the current landscape. Instead of viewing different frameworks and reporting ideas as competing or contradictory, a more comprehensive approach is to examine the entirety of the work. Specifically, there are several trends in the market in addition to the work, research, and advocacy performed by the IIRC, which support the dissemination and reporting of different types of information. Several of these reporting frameworks, although developed by a variety of institutions at different time periods, contain fundamental similarities important for the analysis of integrated reporting.

The Sustainability Accounting Standards Board (SASB), a 501(c) (3) nonprofit organization, is a complementary working group that has generated alternative and additional sustainability reporting frameworks and information. Sustainability information and operating in an environmentally friendly manner represent a growing concern for management professionals across industry lines. The coordination between the SASB research team, industry participants and experts, and regulators that use this information mirrors the inclusive and stakeholder-oriented model of decision-making so important in the global business environment. Specifically, linking together the work performed by the SASB with the integrated reporting framework, an underlying value add of this framework is the standardization and consistency espoused by both frameworks.

Some evidence suggests regulators and external users view these frameworks as competing options in the market, but several similarities benefit users regardless of which options is implemented. First, quantifying different types of information and data linked to sustainability or other types of organizational data is a cornerstone of dynamic decision-making and stakeholder engagement. Codifying just how to report and communicate these different types of information and data in a familiar format is critically important to achieving broader implementation and buy-in across industry lines. Second, again representing some swapping of ideas and concepts between both frameworks is the construction of the business case for nonfinancial information. Management professionals must be able to explain and justify the underlying business case and purpose of reporting these varying data streams, in other words, how will doing so assist the value creation process? Building this bridge and connecting reporting to actually generating stakeholder value is a fundamental part of both frameworks.

Additional support and insights are also available from the work and research currently underway at global professional accounting associations, including the AICPA, IMA, and the International Federation of Accountants (IFAC). Professional accounting organizations have published numerous attestation frameworks and standards to assist with the reporting and communicating of different information to stakeholders. The specifics of these attestation frameworks will differ from organization to organization, but the fact that different accounting organizations are publishing them is encouraging. Such standardization and publishing of frameworks by professional organizations sends a strong signal to market participants that these are not simply trends, but a paradigm shift in reporting information.

This shift indicates a change in not only what types of information are reported to stakeholder groups, but also the pace at which this information is communicated. Added to the standardization of nonfinancial information embedded in these frameworks is the trend of digitization sweeping through the accounting profession. Since accounting and other financial professionals will, in virtually every situation, be the professionals tasked with preparing these comprehensive financials, such awareness and buy-in is important. Leveraging the advances and changes in technology and technological systems available to management professionals also enables the transition from static reporting to dynamic and virtually continuous reporting. Professional associations have also published assurance and attestation frameworks focusing on cybersecurity, internal control systems, and the intersection of technology, accounting, and reporting.

Taking a step back and examining the business case for an integrated reporting framework, the connection between cybersecurity issues and the need from greater attestation standards becomes apparent. As the adoption and implementation rate for nonfinancial and more comprehensive reporting continues to increase, the need for professional input on attestation and assurance will only grow. Circling back to one of the underlying issues integrated reporting attempts to solve, namely the lack of standardization and consistency with regards to nonfinancial information, professional accounting professionals may be able to lend professional expertise and guidance. In order for a more comprehensive type of reporting to gain a toehold, the information and data contained within these frameworks must be compared and analyzed in a familiar format. Developing attestation standards and assurance frameworks to assist practitioners in developing reports and best practices linked to these different streams of information is a significant step toward increasing adoption.

While the need for greater consistency and standardization with regard to nonfinancial and operational data is not a new development, the method by which integrated reporting approaches this issue provides a definitive solution. The multiple capital model, which will be examined in greater detail in the following chapter, presents a platform and methodology for quantitatively reporting and analyzing different amounts of information. Framing different amounts of information in the form of capital also generates a psychological benefit for management professionals seeking to understand and implement an integrated reporting model. The concept of capital, namely the resources and tools at the disposal of management to achieve organizational objectives certainly includes the environmental, operational, and intellectual capital issues embedded within an integrated reporting framework. Put another way, in order to achieve the financial results and objectives desired by management and external analysts, these different types of data must be reported and quantified and reported to internal and external users.

Drilling Down on Integrated Reporting

Integrated Reporting: An Analysis of the Multiple Capital Model

There are numerous reporting frameworks that exist in the marketplace, but one of the most defining factors of integrated reporting is the multiple capital model. For implementation steps and initiatives underway by management professionals seeking to convey the value of the changes necessary to complete this transition, this concept is essential. Communicating information in a quantitative manner, and being able to present and analyze data from operations in a manner familiar and consistent with current reporting, provides an important jumping off point for further discussion. In addition to presenting information in a quantitative framework, the underlying purpose of a multiple capital model is also linked directly to the case of long-term value creation. Drilling down to the purpose of the multiple capital model, and connecting these items to the higher-level issue of developing value for long-term stakeholders, this model provides an effective platform.

Embedded in the very proposition of a multiple capital model, it is important to also recognize what, specifically, the purpose of the model actually represents. The purpose of this model is to deliver information to both internal and external stakeholders while also capturing the increasingly varied nature of what exactly capital represents. Capital, in a traditional interpretation and reporting process represents the financial resources and flows management has at their disposal to fulfill specific organizational objectives. Echoing this traditional definition, the primary focus of financial reporting and external analyses are the familiar financial statistics and metrics. Earnings per share, net income, cash flow metrics, and growth rates over comparable periods all fall under the umbrella of capital analysis. This view, however, is an incomplete and partial view of what capital means for an organization and long-term strategic planning. In order to fulfill strategic objectives and to meet the financial goals and objectives of management, the entire organization must function as one. Operational activities must be proceeding on plan, management must be able to communicate effectively with stakeholders, and financing must be available to sustain operations.

The importance of this multiple capital model, both to the concept of integrated reporting and creating a mindset of long-term value creation, is difficult to overstate. Time and again, one of the fundamental flaws and gaps in current nonfinancial reporting options is the lack of consistency and standardization in said frameworks. Even with industry wide effort and focus, supported by organizations such as the SASB and professional accounting organizations, this deficit has only been partially addressed. Assurance and attestation standards, although important for consistent reporting and adoption by different organizations, are not as helpful for management professionals seeking to implement integrated reporting on an internal basis. Industry specific standards, such as those developed by the SASB, certainly add value to the management conversation but may not provide the action steps necessary for initial adoption and analysis. Approaching this conversation from a quantitative manner, and doing so in a way that connects the goals of the MCM to current operational realities is another proactive aspect of the MCM.

Technology and the MCM

This discussion would be remiss without, at the very least, a brief conversation and discussion about the impact and influence of technological advancements on the ability of organizations to create and communicate nonfinancial information. While this might seem like a primarily technical differentiation and conversation, it has a fundamental impact on the likelihood of success. Analytics and artificial intelligence, building on the previous iterations of big data analysis sweeping the marketplace, continue to provide organizations and management teams with more access to more information on a continuous basis. In order to effectively implement the MCM, and connecting the MCM idea to both integrated reporting and financial reporting, two steps must be taken by teams in different organizations. First, employees should be trained and educated on how to use these different tools and understand the connection between the tools themselves and the MCM goal of the organization. Second, the different technology options available to organizations and management teams must be assessed in an objective manner, without management simply using whichever tool appears to be the most current iteration of technological advancement.

Prior to analyzing this specific connection and linkage between the components of the MCM and the goals of management to report more comprehensive information, it is worthwhile to return to the underlying purpose of this framework. Put simply, the current status of financial reporting is insufficient for the majority of recipients who spend time and efforts examining this information. Although this does not come as a shock or surprise to most management professionals, addressing this information gap is easier said than done in most circumstances. Whether it is due to legacy technology systems, conservatism of management with regard to changing reporting, or the reality that reporting requirements are often an afterthought, making substantial changes to reporting processes can be difficult. Connecting this current situation, with awareness of the problem but a lack of a quantitative framework to address the needs of stakeholders, highlights the true differentiating factors of the multiple capital model.

Implementing the different technology systems and processes necessary to integrate the different sources of information may ultimately require the implementation of different application programming interfaces (APIs) to facilitate the transition and communication of information. Thinking of APIs in terms of portals or virtual doors to bridge the gaps between different technology systems appears to be an appropriate analogy to understand what value is offered by these tools. On the surface, this may seem like yet another complicated technology function to be purchased, debugged, and involving employee training; however, the underlying reality is this technology is already widespread in the market. If an organization has multiple ERP systems already in place, shares certain information with industry partners or suppliers, or connects systems in any way the odds are APIs are used to drive these connections. Framed in that context, the idea of integrated reporting simply represents an extension and evolution of current technologies being applied to emerging areas.

Changing organizational processes and procedures requires, in virtually every situation, a framework and quantitative approach understandable to management; integrated reporting is not an exception to this rule. In order to avoid being classified as yet another reporting or compliance tool, however, any new reporting tool or platform must also be able to deliver value to the management professionals using it. Building this bridge and connection between implementation of integrated reporting across industry lines, and the action steps to actually do so, is a gap addressed by the multiple capital model. The ability to quantify, analyze, and consistently report the multiple stream of information and capital to internal management and external users represents the true value add of the MCM. Addressing the concerns of management is paramount when proposing a new reporting and information system for utilization within the firm. Taking a look at some specific examples of the multiple capital framework is a logical next step, both to assist with proposing this system and making the necessary investments to do so.

Examples of the Different Types of Capital

Circling back to the ideas and concepts embedded within the multiple capital model is important, even after understanding the concepts at a high level, due to the importance this model plays in the implementation of integrated reporting at large. Previously in this book, the concepts and use cases of the different types of capital were analyzed and form the basis for understanding and creating applications. This discussion builds on that earlier dialogue, reinforces the importance and fundamentals of these different capital models, and also highlights how these capitals are actually already being utilized in the marketplace.

Financial Capital

Beginning with financial capital seems reasonable, since this is the class and type of capital management professionals are most familiar with given the current environment. In addition to analyzing standard metrics such a return on investment, return on equity, net income data, and the highly scrutinized earnings per share figures, integrated reporting should also include sources of capital as they relate to the strategic planning process. A simple example might be to include information linked to current financial inflows and outflows in place at the organization to projects and initiatives outlined in the narrative section of the financial statements. Although this information usually is referenced, emphasizing the long-term planning thinking and process underway at the organization is of increasing interest to stakeholder groups. Financial capital may represent the class of capital and information most often analyzed and reported to both internal and external stakeholders, but there should be a balance between shorter-term metrics and information published with a longer-term view in mind.

Examples: Clearly financial information is the most recognized and analyzed type of capital in the marketplace, but taking into account the mission of a multiple capital model highlights the connection between finance and longer-term growth. Ratios and illustrations of these different types of information include, but are not limited to the following type of information. Specifically, comparing an analysis between cash flow statements, buybacks, and reinvestment into research and development are commonly reported metrics, but reveal more about the organization than simply financial performance. Although this does not represent a direct connection between short term and longer-term financial performance, there is evidence that stock repurchases and buybacks do not generally generate longer-term value for stakeholders. Monitoring, and disclosing the long-term plan of management as a part of the information published in both the managerial summary and expanded throughout the report, this represents a quantitative first step organizations can take, and do so using current information and reporting guidelines.

Social and Relational Capital

When the concept of social capital is mentioned in the realm of business development and management, the core idea and concept often refers to social media almost exclusively. It is true that social media provides a powerful platform for management to communicate and disseminate the initiatives and ideas underway at the organization, and to do so on a continuous basis. That said, and this is an important point to emphasize in a stakeholder environment, social media cannot be viewed as simply a one-way channel and communication platform. Simply posting information and appearing to simply trying to push a certain message without taking into account customer and other market feedbacks is a virtually sure-fire way to garner ill-will and frustration among customers and stakeholder groups. Social media is a potentially game-changing tool for organizations communicating and operating in a stakeholder environment, but it must be treated as an ongoing conversation and dialogue. Additionally, representing a potentially differentiating factor in the context of social media management are organizations that not only engage with customers on social media, but who actually connect this feedback to business operations.

Customer service, traditionally, was viewed as a cost center that remained almost unconnected to other business decisions, which often led to substandard service, dissatisfied customers, and damage to organizational reputation. Building on previous themes of globalization, real-time communication, and the instantaneous reach of social media, the importance of customer service for organizational growth cannot be overstated. Integrated reporting has an important role to play in the conversation; as organizations pay more attention and invest more resources in maintaining satisfactory relationships with customers, they must also be able to quantify the impact of these stakeholder relationships. Tracking, analyzing, and creating a feedback loop of stakeholder feedback is an important first step in this process. That said, it is important to recognize that social and relational capital does not only connect to social media platforms.

Example: Reiterating the ability of organizations to begin adapting concepts and components of an integrated reporting framework without requiring substantive investments in new technology or training, it should be noted that social media and communication channels can also become integrated into the reporting structure. For example, taking advantage of customer satisfaction and response information already monitored internally, organizations can rank and report quite simply how well the organization is doing in satisfying customers. Additionally, from an institutional level, management can take a proactive approach with stakeholders and other large investors groups to, in theory, potentially head off activist campaigns, which can quickly grow into distractions for management.

Intellectual Capital

Although this topic was approached and analyzed previously in this research, the growing importance of intangible assets and intellectual property to organizational value is undeniable. With a significant percentage of organizational value linked to intangible assets rising over the last several decades, as industrial economies have evolved into post-industrial or service-based economies, this is no longer just a qualitative manner that can be delegated to a simple footnote disclosure. Granted, the statistics and information related to the amounts and funds invested in research and development are already reported and distributed to external stakeholders, but an integrated reporting framework provides an opportunity to expand this reporting.

For example, as a component of an integrated report the organization can, in addition to publishing and comparing the amounts invested in research and development, include any patents obtained or in process during the year, thus more granularity is now possible. Significant disclosures linked to breakthroughs accomplished at the organization, what percentage of share value is linked to intangible assets, and the asset utilization ratio of intangible assets are items that can, and should be, published. It is a widely acknowledged business reality that intangible assets, intellectual capital, and other sources of intellectual property form a key component of organizational strategy, valuation, and how the firm will compete and succeed in the marketplace moving forward. For example, if an organization has a significant stockpile of intangible assets and programs, the financial impact of this value should be disclosed. Additionally, there should be a metric or information relating to how many of these intangible assets are leveraged toward the strategic goals of the firm.

Examples and applications: Expanded on throughout this book is the idea that the true value of an organization is not simply tied to physical assets, current operations, or the prospects for growth in the next quarter or successive quarters. There may be limits as to what exactly can possibly be communicated regarding the intellectual capital and intangible assets of an organization, especially if they are related to copyright and other proprietary information. That said, it is important to take into account the growing importance of intangible assets to the future success of an organization.

Intellectual capital and intellectual property are often thought of in the context of technology organizations, advanced research, or cutting-edge product development; however, it is important to take into account that intellectual capital can, and should, be measured across a wider array of categories. For example, protecting and securing production processes, regardless of the specific goods produced and distributed to consumers can be considered intellectual property and form the basis for competitive advantages moving forward. Additionally, intellectual property can include items such as customer lists, internal procedures for addressing market feedback, and the mechanisms for addressing both challenges and opportunities as they arise. In a business environment increasingly dominated by intellectual processes, digital information, and intangible assets integrated reporting offers an important application moving forward. Stated differently, integrated reporting allows management and organizations as a whole to classify, quantify, and report different classes of information as intellectual capital, and to do so in a business friendly manner.

Manufactured Capital

When manufactured capital is mentioned the notions and ideas that initially come to the mind of many internal and external users of organizational data are physical assets related to the production of physical goods. This perspective, although appearing initially appropriate, only provides an incomplete view of what exactly manufactured capital means for an organization. Even with the growing number of organizations and businesses conducting larger amounts of business in a digital manner, a physical presence is still almost universally required for consumer-facing organizations. Viewed in this context, the concept of manufactured capital is critically important for one such organizations routinely held as an online business at the forefront of innovation and business leadership: Amazon.

Amazon, which has rapidly expanded into a host of business lines and services, is categorized as a technology company and is led by senior management invested in integrating technology into every aspect of the organization. With the implementation of Amazon Web Services, a hosting and business services platform utilized by many organizations including, but not limited to Netflix, the online perception of this organization has been reinforced. That said, and specifically following the acquisition of Whole Foods by Amazon at the end of 2016, the physical footprint of the organization continues to expand. Additionally, and following the expansion of logistical assets to fulfill and expand services to Amazon Prime customers, the importance of logistical and manufactured assets for the continued success of the organization is difficult to overstate.

An additional aspect of manufactured capital worthy of consideration is the reality that many organizations are increasingly investing in additive manufacturing, 3D manufacturing, or manufacturing processes augmented by technology including both artificial intelligence and blockchain applications. Manufacturing need not represent or result in large products or end results, but rather be distributed between traditional and smaller-scale manufacturing is an item that can, and should, be a consideration in the integrated reporting construct. Virtually any organization, regardless of available resources at any given point in time, can engage in the manufacturing process and information communicated within these documents.

Natural Capital

While natural capital may be most closely linked and associated with sustainability initiatives already underway at a number of organizations across industry lines, building the bridge between sustainability ideas and natural capital is something that requires additional investment and initiative by members of the management team. At a high level, the idea of natural capital is an idea and concept that should be a relatively straightforward concept to communicate to different stakeholder groups. Operating in a sustainable manner, and implementing environmentally sensitive and oriented activities is an idea and concept of interest to a number of stakeholder groups. Regulators, consumers, institutional shareholders, and retail investors are increasingly interested in creating a business strategy and plan that creates value in a short, medium, and long term manner.

Quantifying natural capital can, and should, take different forms depending on the industry and organization in question, but a few underlying themes remain consistent regardless of industry orientation or theme. Drilling down specifically into how management teams can report and quantify the results of environmental information and the impact these actions have on financial results, a common trend is to focus resources and personnel into sustainability-oriented projects. Investing in sustainability initiatives and forming a business portfolio of activities generating value over a continuum of timelines all too often fails to generate returns in alignment with other organizational goals. As much as it may appeal to the management and certain stakeholder groups of the organizations to operate in a sustainable manner, financial considerations and variables represent an inevitable part of running a business that is public traded and has stakeholders invested in learning more.

Drilling down specifically, however, reveals some tactics that can be placed into action at a variety of organizations regardless of industry affiliation and orientation. Linking back to the example and market leadership provided by Adidas in the arena of sustainability, natural capital, and managing the different projects provides a blueprint other organizations can follow. For example, an organization engaged in sustainable business operations, such as renewable energy, installing energy efficient assets throughout business operations, or providing consulting services to client organizations in these areas, has a clear mandate for implementing natural capital initiatives in a straightforward manner. It is clear that even organizations that operate in industries only tangentially related to sustainability and natural capital have the ability, and, increasingly, the responsibility to introduce natural capital reporting into the communication process.

Natural capital, viewed from a high level, is linked to sustainability and environmentally oriented operations, but quantifying the impacts of these initiatives can be difficult without the appropriate framework in place. One example that may be appropriate, in an attempt to quantify both the importance and the impact of natural capital reporting and initiatives has to do with organizing the stakeholder environment for reporting purposes. Reporting different types and amounts of information for communicative purposes, however, is not sufficient when attempting to overhaul and fundamentally change just how the entity disseminates initiatives. This may unfortunately fall under the category of greenwashing, which generates ideas and statements meant to assuage stakeholder groups.

Human Capital

The idea of human capital and the intersection between human capital and organization performance might seem more appropriate to classify under human resources than financial reporting. Although this view may traditionally have represented the prevailing wisdom, it only provides an incomplete view of what exactly human capital and information mean for financial performance. Despite the greater integration of technology in business operations and processes, employee training and development are critically important for the continued success of organizations during the medium and long term. This perception and mindset are often repeated by management personnel and external stakeholders, but represents a contradictory position to how these items are classified financially.

Training and development items, much like research and development, are categorized as expenses on the income statement, which in turn has a negative impact on the bottom line. While such an approach is an appropriate technical accounting approach to these items, it does not reflect the importance of employee education and training for sustainable growth and development. One approach that can be implemented at various organizations builds on existing procedures already in place, namely the practice of engagement procedures. Discovering employee interests, talents, and skills is an important tool that management has at its disposal to implement new technology practices. Linking back to the concept of integrated reporting, it is clear that in order to fully implement this new reporting framework, changes and education will be necessary. Human capital, often associated with education, should be something fully integrated into how the strategic planning and reporting process is implemented.

While this topic will be discussed and analyzed in the greater depth throughout this text, it is appropriate to introduce the concept of human capital as it pertains to integrated reporting at this point. Specifically, and this is a fact worthy of emphasis, it is the employees that work at the organization, making specific operational decisions, and crafting strategic plans that are the driving force behind much of the value creation. Even with the proliferation of technology, including but not limited to artificial intelligence and blockchain tools, the importance of management professionals to keep the long-term view in mind is arguably more important than before.

Connection between MCM and Long-Term Value Creation

A theme repeated often by management teams across industry lines is the importance of creating value over the medium and long term for all stakeholders; however, a gap between what is spoken about and what is actually done continues to exist. A focus on financial capital, and the earnings myopia that so often dominates the management dialogue with external stakeholders can result in an organization acting inconsistently with its stated goals. Speaking about generating value in a long-term and sustainable manner is a goal every management team should strive to enact, as it represents a truly competitive advantage. Value creation and communicating the value created over the long term for stakeholders is a fiduciary duty of management professionals regardless of industry affiliation or organizational size. Even though this duty is routinely acknowledged by institutional investors, market analysts, and corporate strategists connecting the proverbial dots between statements and action remains difficult.

Bridging the gap between what is expected of organizations by market analysts and other participants, the goals of nonfinancial stakeholders, and the importance of developing growth for the medium to long term is a challenge in the most stable of business environments. It is not a secret, nor a surprise, that the current business landscape and environment would be classified as anything but stable or consistent in nature. Whether it is focusing on technology, demographic shifts in the workplace, the increased digitization of business information, or the growing importance of nonfinancial information, the importance of juggling short-term expectations and longer-term requirements is arguably more important than previously. That said, and acknowledging the reality that doing so forms a key component of fiduciary duty does change the fact that addressing both of these apparently disparate goals, and something increasingly expected of management professionals.

One of the most difficult tasks of management personnel and the staff reporting to the senior and strategic leadership is quantifying the reporting of the positive and negative implications investment decisions have over a variety of time horizons. Especially when faced with the quarterly grilling by financial and market analysts, the best laid plans and justifications of management can fall flat time and again. The pressure to fulfill or even exceed periodic earnings targets is acute for a variety of reasons and makes sustainably investing for future growth a difficult endeavor. For example, organizations and management professionals often cite the pressure to fulfill and exceed earnings estimates as reasons for cutting investment and employee education initiatives. This behavior continues, even as time and again organizations investing during boom and bust times generate superior returns versus peers and competitors; indeed, without a comprehensive reason for doing so, management may be hard pressed to explain such investments. After all, two of the largest and most important stakeholder groups for any organization publicly traded or privately held are creditors and shareholders. Creditors extend capital and financing to the organization based, almost exclusively, on the calculated probability the organization will be able to fulfill interest payment obligations consistently. Shareholders, in a related manner, are most often interested in the ability of the organization to either continue paying dividends, or the ability to consistently grow earnings in alignment with market expectations.

Having a template and reporting structure in place to help narrate and explain the implications of long-term investments and value creation is critical to adopting, and sustaining the adoption of integrated reporting. Without a robust framework and narrative explanation for undertaking certain actions, the management team will revert to traditional behavior to fulfill traditional expectations at the first sign of a drop in profitability or cash flow. Integrated reporting, and specifically the multiple capital model, enables management to defend and justify doing what—from a strict financial perspective—may appear to be illogical decisions. Making said investments, however, are what provide and lay the foundations for growth in the medium and long term. Communicating the strategic nature of financial investments, constructing an understandable business narrative for stakeholders to understand, and following up with quantitative results is a management imperative. In addition to creating a template for communication and information distribution, having a standardized framework and reporting structure also enables the types of data being communicated to be compared and tracked over different periods of time.

This most recent point, the ability of management to consistently follow-up and refine initial positions related to strategic investments is an idea that is arguably more important than the initial statement itself. While not as splashy as simply announcing the implementation of new strategies or tactics, the tactical and daily follow-ups associated with new communication is an important part of sustainable adoption. Grand statements, press releases, and an upfront push to support a specific investment decision is a logical and reasonable way to launch a strategic initiative, but maintaining buy-in and momentum is essential. All too often, long-term decisions and actions undertaken with a longer-term perspective can lose mindshare of employees and stakeholders due to the fact that the pay horizon is going to be in the medium and long term by default. Once again, the reality of quarterly or other periodic earnings announcement places the management team under a tremendous amount of pressure to fulfill these goals. Put simply, instead of focusing on leveraging current successes to plant the seeds of future growth, organizations and management professionals are universally occupied with satisfying short-term needs of the marketplace.

A multiple capital framework assists in maintaining this focus on long-term development and value creation because management has the platform and language to communicate effectively with stakeholders. Identifying and ranking the different classes of capital available to management professionals highlights the importance of said capitals to stakeholder groups, and helps management connect investments to capital with the long-term plan of the organization. A connection like this, a comprehensive understanding of how different management actions will influence the organization moving forward connects both to integrated reporting and the need for a more comprehensive reporting framework. Building this bridge between where the organization is in the competitive landscape versus where the firms wants to be should form the basis of stakeholder engagement across industry lines. Drilling down specifically into one such area, a linkage between integrated reporting, a multiple capital model, and the concept of blue ocean strategy becomes apparent.

Blue Ocean and Integrated Reporting

To present a brief and high-level analysis of the concept, a blue ocean strategy can be summarized as a tactic for an organization to redefine the rules and norms by which it competes in respective industries. Upon doing this, the organization will find itself competing in a blue ocean, with much reduced competition and price pressures, versus traditional red oceans defined almost exclusively by price and margin pressures. Clearly the idea of making such a pivot is appealing to management professionals, but the path to achieve this objective can be difficult to complete while balancing the numerous other objectives on the proverbial management plate. Integrated reporting, by the very nature of the reporting template, encourages management and the professional stakeholder community to take a more comprehensive view of where firms are positioned, and their tactics moving forward.

Creating new markets and business opportunities lies at the core of the blue ocean strategy idea, and has remained a consistent pillar of the management philosophy since it was introduced to the management landscape in the early 2000s. Generating new value and opportunities clearly represents a fiduciary responsibility of management professionals regardless of industry affiliation, but doing so can be extremely difficult given market pressures and forces. Strategy and the strategic planning process is not a process by itself, nor an idea that is lacking in substance, support, or quantitative structure but may be a component of management philosophy limiting potential opportunities and insights. Much like how introducing certain arguments and ideas in a verbal conversation can restrict the bandwidth or conversation and debate, focusing only on existing product and service offerings limits the lens through which the organization views the marketplace.

Blue ocean strategy—virtually by default of the design of the methodology— tasks management professionals with developing new products, services, and ways to enter the marketplace. Connecting this idea, which may initially appear to simply represent yet another management protocol, with the underlying quantitative data that inevitably drives business decision-making is a challenge, and is an area integrated reporting can possibly address. New business lines and opportunities, however, are often driven and generated from a better analysis and understanding of both current information and how to glean insights from the changing nature of data streams. Prior to this idea being actualized, however, it is important to conduct a comprehensive analysis of both current and projected ideas and opportunities, including those that may build off of nonfinancial data.

Performing a comprehensive analysis of the current competitive positioning of the organization is clearly important for management professionals, but the following step of projecting future strategy is arguably more important. At the core of the idea, blue ocean strategy, and engaging a shift toward implementing a blue ocean strategy, necessitates an overhaul and change in how management deals with information and messaging. Summarizing this concept in a relatively concise manner, the underlying idea is that organizations must understand the core competencies of the organization and how it is perceived by customers. While the ideas postulated in the blue ocean framework are oriented toward better engagement with customers, this can easily be augmented to a stakeholder-based model of engagement.

Connecting together the concept of blue ocean strategy with integrated reporting reveals a key insight and upside of adopting integrated reporting, and it should be a part of the conversation. As part of the implementation process, which will be examined in more depth in following chapters, management teams will inevitable obtain greater insights into how the organization operates and manages different streams of information. In order to obtain these insights and benefits, however, integrated reporting cannot simply be layered on top of existing systems. Rather, integrated reporting systems and processes must be treated as a comprehensive change to how information is processed and treated in the strategic planning process. Outlining action steps, that are taken should involve technology, strategy, and finance functions.

Of course, simply stating there should be a connection between integrated reporting, strategic planning, and the idea of blue ocean strategic planning is one item, but it is an entirely different matter to execute and transition this idea into business-oriented action steps. Integrated reporting requires a variety of changes in both how an organization produces information and how this information is communicated to external stakeholder groups. While this might not immediately look like it connects to the idea of strategic planning, upon closer review the connection and action steps become clear. Generating and analyzing this greater variety of information, communicating these data to external users, and using this information to help create more comprehensive plans requires a shift in how management professionals view both the organization in the present, and how they will be moving forward. Assembling these different flows of information, and viewing the marketplace in a more comprehensive way may very well open up opportunities not regularly available or that were part of routine management analysis.

Chapter 5

Integrated Reporting: Implementation Challenges and Opportunities

Even after analyzing some of the leading organizations currently using integrated financial reporting, there is still the reality of implementation on an organization to organization basis. While the benefits—both financial and operational—that can be generated and associated with the adoption and gradual implementation of a comprehensive reporting framework are evident from a market analysis, the process must nevertheless be undertaken by management. As with any large-scale change or evolution, even if rolled out on a gradual basis or in iterative stages, there are challenges and opportunities that accompany this change. Chapter 5 breaks down the different aspects, areas, and venues through integrated reporting that can be introduced, discussed, and analyzed from an internal basis. Internal discussions, especially when associated with change and change management can be difficult, so entering this conversation with a framework and plan can help address the inevitable stumbling blocks that arise.

Implementation of Integrated Reporting: Internal

Any large change to reporting and communication processes will invariably require changes, upgrades, and modifications to how the organization treats and processes information. It would be remiss to discuss the implementation of integrated financial reporting without acknowledging the technology requirements and upgrades necessary to do so. At the core of the integrated reporting concept lay two fundamental ideas. First, in order to construct a strategic and quantitative narrative around which the organization can grow, management must understand what is occurring at the firm. Although the advances in technology, analytics, and processing systems continue to advance and develop at an accelerating rate, much of organizational information is not harnessed and utilized effectively. Simply having the information produced within the organization is insufficient. All too often, different components and operating groups within the company invest, operate, and analyze information in a manner akin to siloed operations, which is insufficient in a global and digitized environment.

Second, and imperative to sustain the strategic plan and narrative constructed by management, the management team at various levels within the firm must be able to communicate and discuss this information with stakeholder groups. Obtaining buy-in, both internally and externally, is critical to sustaining both the initial adoption of integrated reporting and the continued utilization of said framework. Technology upgrades and changes will inevitably play a large role in facilitating this conversation, but an important point to acknowledge is that many of the tools and information necessary are already available. At the same time, however, it is critical that other operational constructs are taken into account with regards to building and maintaining an integrated reporting framework (Figure 5.1).

It is difficult to overstate just how important the breaking down of silos is for the successful implementation of integrated reporting. At the core of the idea, and emphasized by some of the organizations examined in this text, is that integrated reporting requires coordination and cooperation among virtually all aspects of an organization. Thinking longer term, embracing a strategic shift in

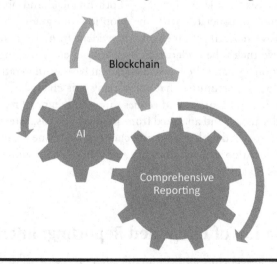

Figure 5.1   Connecting technology trends to changing reporting trends.

how the organization operates and reporting a variety of nonfinancial information in addition to financial will simply happen on its own; management must take action steps to make this reality occur. One of the key hurdles, both internally and externally, is communicating both the intent of the organization and the benefits of operating in this manner. Ensuring a continuous flow of information and data between stakeholder groups is an imperative for management professionals seeking to implement this methodology.

Drilling in specifically to the different changes and modifications necessary is an important part of the integrated reporting process and must be taken into account when analyzing the steps necessary to do so. Even with the increased integration of technology through different management disciplines, it is important to understand that the implementation of integrated reporting within an organization requires a robust internal dialogue to initiate the conversation and sustain the adoption of this new framework. Technology plays a role in any organizational initiative or project, but it is important to make sure that although technology plays a larger role in business it is only a tool in the management toolbox.

Technology Requirements

The core value of integrated reporting is, first, the quantification of various types of information already in existence in the organization. Second, and building on the quantification of said streams of information, is the methods by which this information and data are communicated to different stakeholder groups. Third, and perhaps the most interesting aspect of the integrated reporting framework, is that this information must be linked into the strategic planning process. In order to facilitate this implementation and quantification of information technology upgrades, advancements and investments must be made to utilize existing information effectively. The upside to management professionals and other personnel employed by an organization is that both the information necessary for integrated reporting and the technology systems necessary to do so in real-time already exist in many larger organizations.

Whether it is the IoT, advanced analytics, artificial intelligence, the adoption of blockchain technology tools and platforms by different organizations in the marketplace, the trend is clear. Analytics, the more sophisticated utilization of organizational data, and the real-time availability of said information play ever-larger roles in how organizations are managed. Harnessing this information, whether it is specifically linked to customer service initiatives, supply chain logistics, stakeholder initiatives and activist investors, financial returns on sustainability projects, or other types of strategic plans underway, is critical to the success of an organization in the medium and long term. Data and digital assets have repeatedly been referred to as the most important assets of the twenty-first century, and making effective use of said information is a management imperative.

Artificial intelligence and blockchain are two of the most high profile technology tools currently forming the core of market attention and analysis, and they can play a significant role in the creation of a hospitable environment for integrated reporting. At the core of the idea underlying the enthusiasm surrounding these technology tools is the reality that both technologies enable management teams and organizations to make better use of information already produced within the firm. Information is clearly already used by management in a variety of projects and ideas, but the transition from periodic to real-time analysis and reporting can also assist technology projects and adoption of a more comprehensive information framework.

Analyzing specifically the steps that might be taken via investments in technology, the most appropriate place to begin is to understand what types of information are reported, what stakeholders are communicated with, and what types of information are distributed to these different stakeholder groups. Taking the broader and higher level perspective on this issue is important to avoid getting lost in the proverbial weeds and enables a clear enunciation and justification for technology investments and training. Forming the correct narrative is critical, especially since any changes and modifications to the technology platforms and tools at the organization can cause friction and generate pushback from internal groups. After obtaining the necessary strategic headset and associated insights, specific tactics and approaches will be appropriate. Specifically, several steps and insights appear to be reasonable and logical given this backdrop.

First, a review of existing systems should be conducted, running in the background and not dominating the time of assigned employees. Coordinating different enterprise systems and ensuring comparability between ledgers and informational systems are relatively straightforward ways to initiate this conversation. Even if an organization is not particularly interested in adopting integrated reporting at this juncture or is engaged in a different strategic planning process, conducting this review is important. Coordinating the flow of information throughout the organization, from point of sales information generated by customers to inventory restocking and management issues, all the way to the necessary financing to purchase said inventory, is the backbone of competition in the increasingly digital environment. A common stumbling block that hamstrings organizations, at various stages of growth and development, and in different industries, is that different internal technology systems do not talk to each other. Bridging this gap and understanding the potential negative implications of having data systems that do not function appropriately is somewhere any initiative should begin.

Second, simply acknowledging this reality is merely a starting point and conducting this review, engaging a variety of stakeholder groups, and initiating an analysis of technology platforms are other important starting points. Integrated reporting—by its very nature—changes the variety and type of information disseminated and requires comprehensive dialogue between internal stakeholder groups. Obtaining buy-in from a variety of internal functions and departments, who will all play a significant role in the success or failure of the integrated reporting initiative, is facilitated by early and consistent dialogue. Subsequent to this initial analysis and conversation related to the current state of technology infrastructure, pain points, potential opportunities, and stumbling blocks to said opportunities can be identified and brought into the open. Such transparency and candor both reflect an underlying goal of integrated reporting and a benefit of operating in a stakeholder-oriented manner.

Technology Regulation

A conversation about technology in the current market environment would be incomplete without a mention of technology regulation, specifically the General Data Protection Regulation (GDPR) recently introduced and rolled out by the European Union in May of 2018. While this legislation has been underway since 2016, the finalization of this law in 2018, after several years of data breaches and corporate information breaches, appears to be uniquely timely for the moment, as of this writing, due to the emphasis GDPR places on the connection between different types of information and the impact data have on organizational performance. Specifically, and without diving too much into the weeds of what exactly this regulation entails, there are several key characteristics that make this regulation important for management professionals across industry lines. While not meant to be exhaustive nor all-inclusive, the following short list of applicable components should play a role in the decision-making process:

1. GDPR is a global regulation and even though the GDPR originated in the EU, the very nature of information means that, in essence, if an organization does business with any EU citizen or organization that handles EU citizenry information it will fall under the umbrella of the GDPR. This is especially pertinent as the fines and mandates embedded within the regulation, including a potential fine of up to 4% of revenue (turnover in the original parlance), mean this law has enforceability clauses as well as recommendations.

2. Large amounts and types of information are covered and the core intention of the GDPR, as per publicly available statements and information, is to provide better and more comprehensive safeguards for consumer information; however, it does not mean it only applies to social media types of information. Much of the financial information collected by organizations, including but not limited to payment information, purchase history, and engagements with an organization through communication channels is considered personal information in the context of the GDPR.

3. It will have an impact on blockchain implementation, as blockchain technology, regardless of the specific industry in question, is already having a dramatic impact on how different organizations operate and do business. That said, some of the core characteristics and benefits associated with

blockchain technology, including the permanence of blockchain data and the instantaneous transmission of information to network members, may cause friction with GDPR implementation. This will be something virtually every organization will have to be aware of and take into account moving forward.

4. GDPR implementation is just beginning. GDPR has been rolled out in May 2018 but the increased focus and scrutiny on how organizations will handle confidential and potentially sensitive information is a conversation that will only become more important over time. As different stakeholder groups, including consumer advocacy and environmental groups continue to obtain access to and exercise influence over management teams, the importance of a comprehensive data strategy will only grow in importance.

5. It treats information as the asset it is; what perhaps is the most striking feature of the GDPR is that, virtually for the first time in a regulatory construct, data and organizational information is being treated, classified, and regulated like an organizational asset. By regulating what organizations do with the information they have access to and control over, regulators are, in effect, treating organizational data like other intangible assets. Integrated reporting with an increased focus on classifying, quantifying, and reporting different streams of organizational data and information seems to be in close alignment with this mindset.

It is true that GDPR implementation is still in the early stages and there remains quite a bit of uncertainty with regard to just how this regulation will (1) be implemented in the marketplace and (2) ultimately impact different types of organizations. It is clear that with the passage of the law organizational data, regardless of whether it is obtained internally of from external sources will face increased scrutiny and focus in the near future. Data are ultimately what drive the organizational decision-making process, and in order to make the most effective decisions for an organization, management professionals must have access to, and clear operating guidelines for, how to treat, classify, report, and safeguard different classes of information.

Additionally, and arguably more important than any specific regulation or law passed related to information regulation, is the transition and evolution in how data are treated by both management professionals and the broader business community. Blockchain technology is perhaps the most buzzworthy technology currently entering the marketplace but it is merely one example of how different technological forces are disrupting the business landscape. Artificial intelligence, cryptocurrencies, machine learning, and the increased used of data analytics across industry and company lines represent powerful steps forward, reflecting just how important data are for organizational success. This transition from passive data collection to preliminary data analysis and reporting, as well as to active machine learning and data crunching on a continuous basis has not gone unnoticed by either the market or regulators.

Market actors have sought to leverage this increasingly rich source of competitive information whereas regulators have, up until very recently, been playing catch up as organizations invest in these areas. Integrated reporting is merely one example of how the increased availability of information is changing business practices, how data are communicated, and what stakeholders expect of organizations with regards to information production. As more information becomes digitized, however, and larger amounts of it are available to different users groups, regulatory attention and focus will inevitably increase. Looking onwards, it will be interesting to observe not only how this regulatory attention impacts the technical data side of the business, but how this regulatory focus will drive changes and transitions in the reporting environment as well.

Operational Requirements

Even with the integration of technology into virtually every aspect of business and management decision-making, it remains a tool of management and not a driving force for decision-making. Revamping and overhauling the reporting and information communication process at an organization inevitably requires that operational functions and decisions also change and evolve. Attempting to layer a comprehensive and stakeholder-oriented reporting structure and process atop of existing silos, pain points, and internal political turf wars present in an organization is a recipe for frustration and failure. This again highlights the importance of early and consistent dialogue and engagement with a variety of internal stakeholders. No matter what industry or position in the current competitive landscape, every business is subject to the same dramatic changes in the marketplace, which continually disrupt incumbent firms. Digitization, the role of artificial intelligence in the analytics and decision-making process, global competition, and political uncertainty simply add to the complexity of managing and running an organization.

Technology is a quantitative tool and platform, which will require investment, training, and other management focus to assist in the implementation process—but that is only a portion of the story. Quantitative data analysis, specifically as it pertains to the insights and applications possible with the rapid advances in technology is difficult to understate in the current marketplace. Artificial intelligence, for example, will enable management professionals at different levels within an organization to eventually make sense and process the possibly overwhelming amounts of information produced by the organization. Compounding the almost supercharged processing ability possible (with the growing implementation of AI platforms and technology) are the implications associated with blockchain technology. Blockchain, specifically the real-time and instantaneous nature of the data uploaded and verified onto the platform itself enables more efficient reporting and analysis, including communicating these insights to stakeholder groups.

Despite the reality that technology is a quantitative platform and tool, a qualitative training and narrative is both expected and required to ensure a smooth implementation of different technologies within the organization. Establishing a framework and narrative around the implementation of technology tools is essential, both from an employee perspective and to ensure stakeholders understand the implications of technology for the organization. For example, employees within an organization may initially generate pushback or resistance to new technology platforms by linking it to job automation and possible job force reduction. Explaining the underlying purpose of the implementation of tools and platforms such as AI, big data platforms and analytics, including blockchain and possibly other technology is essential toward establishing buy-in and ensuring a sustainable implementation.

For example, if the strategic planning process currently in place at the organization is, for all intents and purposes, managed by a small subset of employees, this presents both a challenge and opportunity for improvement. A siloed approach may certainly function and in fact may have been cited as a reason for success and execution of previous initiatives, but only pertains to a limited set of stakeholders and objectives. Circling back to the previous discussion and analysis of traditional reporting, in order to change this process it requires the breaking down of organizational silos. Specifically, facilitating the changes necessary for successful implementation of integrated reporting means that a variety of stakeholder groups and personnel will have to be involved in this decision-making process. Coordinating the various personnel, politics, and resource constraints in place at every organization necessitates that management will, inevitably, have to play a proactive role in this implementation process. While the technology systems and processes play a large role in this conversation, the underlying processes and problems already in place at the organization will not be overcome with additional technological complications. Redefining the roles and responsibilities of individual functional groups, and ensuring different functional groups understand the purpose of these changes represents another internal dialogue management professionals should be having within the organization. One functional area in particular, however, appears to be directly impacted by the implementation of integrated reporting throughout the organization—the management accounting function.

Management Accounting Expectations

Mirroring the traditional role of the accounting reporting and analytic process in general, the management accounting function traditionally has held the role of scorekeeper and analyst of historical information. Certainly, the knowledge and expertise that has served accounting professionals in the areas of attest, assurance services, and taxation will continue to form the foundation of the profession moving forward. Taking this into account, however, is neither a reason nor a justification for practitioners or the profession in general to take a lackadaisical approach to the

Figure 5.2 Analytics circling back to both financial and operational KPIs.

changing business environment. Many of the technological and analytical changes that benefit management professionals and organizations are simultaneously causing upheaval within the accounting profession. Artificial intelligence, increasingly scalable analytical tools and platforms, and the increased integration of blockchain into supply chains and logistical operations necessitate change in the profession. Put simply, there are few roles within an organization, or a functional group of professionals, posed to change as dramatically as the management accounting function (Figure 5.2).

This may strike some readers of this text as strange or unusual, but the accounting function has a critical role to play in the successful development and implementation of integrated reporting. Organizational choices and management decisions are, at the end of the day, driven and governed by quantitative information usually prepared and reported by the accounting function. Obtaining buy-in and support for the necessary internal changes to implement integrated reporting from accounting professionals is an important step that cannot be overlooked. Quantifying and reporting various amounts of information and data form core competencies of the profession currently, and will have practitioners fulfill expectations of the accounting profession moving forward. This is clearly not the only connection between integrated reporting and accounting, but the increased standardization increases the usefulness of this nonfinancial information and ensures better assurance and attestation standards in this area.

Clearly the quantification and reporting of information are essential steps for both accounting professionals and the success or failure of integrated financial reporting. As important as it is for management to consistently work to integrate different operational and technology functions, bringing finance and accounting into this conversation is equally as important. All too often, finance and accounting professionals and teams are brought into the conversation at the conclusion of the decision-making process and are only tasked with, in essence, reviewing the mathematical veracity of the projections. Not only does this not fully utilize the competencies and talents of the finance and accounting function—and limit insights possible by said professionals, but it also limits the likelihood of achieving buy-in. Integrating the financial and accounting functions throughout the other processes is logical because, at a fundamental level, changes in how an organization reports and communicates information falls under the umbrella of these functional groups. Additionally, management accounting professionals and the internal finance function already have substantial experience with analyzing, quantifying, and explaining the various streams of information produced by a firm. Building on these changes, the next logical aspect and area to transform and adapt are the underlying communication and processes, that is, how to present these changes to an external environment.

In case the implications of an integrated report remain unclear or are possibly still open to interpretation by some market analysts, the potential disruption of the management accounting function are significant. First, expanding the scope of information that may fall under the scope and functional expertise of the accounting function generates opportunities for accounting professionals to collaborate with additional external stakeholder groups on a continuous basis. Partnering with other internal groups may seem like a routine extension of accounting work, but it represents a fundamental shift in how the profession is perceived both internally and externally. Second, is the increased integration of technology within the accounting process, which plays a leading role in how the profession is perceived and viewed by colleagues and external partners. While organizations at large continue to grapple with the implications of greater technology integration, few professions stand to be as disrupted or influenced by technology than accounting. The specifics may vary from organization to organization and may include simply automating base level tasks to begin the process, but these fundamental steps represent what is necessary to generate the action-oriented data necessary for stakeholder engagement. Such an engagement also represents an important function that improved and more timely quantitative information can fulfill.

Chapter 6

Implementation of Integrated Reporting: External

Rolling out and implementing an integrated reporting framework is a comprehensive change, both in mindset and operational reality, in how an organization operates, quantifies, and reports data generated by an organization. As if management professionals were not already juggling with a host of internal pressures and forces when attempting to lead management initiatives for change, there is the reality that when changing how data are reported to external stakeholders there will inevitably be some pushback from market participants. Especially in service-based economies and postindustrial markets, there is a tremendous pressure brought to bear on organizations to meet, or even exceed quarterly financial targets projected and estimated by the market. Changing this conversation, and implementing a paradigm shift between organizations, market analysts, and actors is an essential ingredient in successfully implementing and sustaining an integrated reporting framework. Put simply, it is all too easy to lose focus on longer-term value creation if quarterly earnings targets are missed, so this may require substantial changes in how often data are released to market participants. Chapter 6 delves into not only identifying how to begin this transition, but also how different factors must be taken into account when dealing with different stakeholder groups interested in different aspects of organizational performance.

Clearly, organizations and management teams seeking to implement an integrated reporting framework must engage in a comprehensive dialogue internally, but this is only half of the necessary debate. Especially for organizations under scrutiny with regards to earnings figures and profitability (such as publicly traded entities), this is a stumbling block that can potentially derail the integrated reporting process. Akin to the importance of engaging various stakeholder groups internally in a consistent manner from the very beginning, it is imperative external stakeholders also be involved in this conversation. While certain stakeholder groups, namely environmental and nongovernmental entities, should be supporters of a more comprehensive and holistic view of financial performance, other traditional shareholder groups might not be as enthusiastic. Developing a comprehensive conversation, engaging with different stakeholder groups, and doing so on an ongoing basis is critical to achieving external buy-in. Critical to this conversation, however, is the importance and almost necessary development of guiding frameworks and metrics.

Circling back to the underlying construct and framework of integrated reporting as it pertains to the business environment, stakeholders—including but not limited to financial shareholders—are interested in the performance of the organization. A key distinction, particularly in the wake of scandals and incidents of corporate malfeasance is to ensure current financial performance is not being obtained at the expense of medium and longer-term performance. Especially as regulatory bodies across industry and geographic lines become more assertive in suggesting replacement and reshuffling of management and directors, ignoring these trends does not represent good business sense. Engaging with stakeholders to ensure the message and platform of integrated reporting is understood, and that the benefits to the organization are quantifiable are important first steps.

This conversation, especially when dealing with market forces including analysts and investment firms focused on periodic earnings estimates and results, also highlights the importance of coordinating with accounting and financial professionals. As proactive and supportive certain stakeholder groups may be for a message of increased sustainability and sustainable growth, decisions and continued success still require quantitative data to support these decisions. Developing reports and ensuring these can be delivered on a consistent basis is an absolute must when establishing these relationships and communication channels.

Stakeholder management, or the development and maintenance of relationships with external user groups of information, is a responsibility and duty of management, which represents a high profile example of an existing duty that will continue to evolve over time. While developing relationships with the market, that is, creditors and providers of equity capital (shareholders) currently occupies a substantial percentage of management time, the scope and approach of this engagement must also evolve and change. The most important piece of this conversation and dialogue is to ensure that different stakeholder groups understand both the short-term and longer realities of integrated reporting on organizational decision-making. Especially for convincing financial shareholders and stakeholders of the importance and validity of this transition, the financial implications of integrated reporting should be linked to the strategic framework of the organization.

While financial investments and decisions made during the implementation phase of integrated reporting may, in the short term, seem contradictory to the periodic earnings and cash flow initiatives underway at the organization, it's important to communicate the other implications of these actions. This apparent contradiction between shorter and longer-term goals of the organization actually appears to be a symptom of a deeper disconnect between what management professionals state as goals, and what organizations actually execute. Stated simply, making investments and strategic decisions will inevitably require that the organization dedicate financial resources to these activities. One common use of capital in the current marketplace, however, is dedicating significant portions of cash flow, or even issuing debt instruments to fund stock dividends or repurchases. Again, while such tactics may be helpful in the short-term, in all likelihood, they do not represent the best long-term use of organizational resources.

Stakeholder Expectations

Acknowledging the reality that in either case the organization is dedicating financial resources and committing the organization to a set of long-term realities, a comparison can now occur between current and projected actions. Taking a high level view of this situation, well over $8 trillion has been spent/invested on corporate share repurchases and increases to dividend activities. Examples abound and include such high profile examples as Apple, Exxon, IBM, and numerous others, which have undertaken such activities to assuage the short-term whims of market participants and actors. The question to focus on, when met with resistance, is to highlight the reality that financial resources and investments will be made in either scenario, but which set of investments is made to generate medium and long-term growth? The development and sustainability of growth in the marketplace requires investments, even if said investments do not generate immediate short-term financial returns.

Managing the expectations of stakeholders, especially financial shareholders, is a critical step in the implementation process for a logical and straightforward reason; these end users can exercise quite large amounts of control over the management process. For example, if shareholders become dissatisfied with either the financial performance of the organization, or the explanations and narratives provided by management to explain approaches to certain market conditions, shareholder-led campaigns could be launched. No organization or management team, regardless of past performance, industry, size, or current levels of profitability is immune from the possibility of activist campaigns. An oft-cited complaint and issue levied against existing management in these situations is that management is not acting in the way or manner that maximizes shareholder value. Maximizing shareholder value is clearly a fiduciary responsibility of management, but creating value for both the organization and shareholders should be viewed in the short, medium, and longer-term contexts (Figure 6.1).

Integrated reporting, by the nature of a more holistic and comprehensive approach to managing an organization and allocating financial resources, aligns

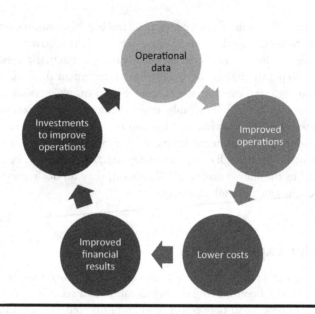

Figure 6.1 Linking integrated reporting to organizational benefits.

with the medium and long-term value creation process. Approaching the situation from a stakeholder-oriented perspective, instead of merely a financial shareholder point of view, allows management to construct a strategic plan and investment strategy aligned with the best interests of stakeholders and shareholders. Taking into account the needs of different stakeholder groups and members also allows management professionals to explain and narrate the strategy and plan of the firm going forward. Management professionals are tasked with both achieving financial goals and objectives of the organization, as well as fulfilling the needs and expectations of the marketplace and different stakeholder groups; an effective communication strategy is core to this goal.

One tactic and idea that has been used by some organizations, with varying levels of success and adoption, is to change the frequency with which information is reported to external users. For example, a common aspect of financial management and the associated fiduciary duty of management teams is that an organization must be able to meet and hopefully exceed whatever financial goals and objectives have been amalgamated from analysts estimates. A strategy that can be implemented as a countervailing trend to analyst estimates is to simply change the parameters for how information is reported to external users, namely by issuing information on a less consistent basis than previously.

Publishing information, whether it is financial or nonfinancial data serves a dual function in the context of data management and market feedback. First, as information is produced, finalized, and reported there are obvious implications management professionals can derive from this process. Namely, and perhaps most obviously, as data are produced, cleaned, and analyzed, management teams can produce insights related to this information. That said, however, the very fact that this information is distributed to other market participants and end users provides external analysts with different types of information to examine and possibly critique. Specifically, this feedback loop and mechanism is often how the best laid plans of an organization, as they pertain to generating medium and long-term growth, can be derailed by one or several short-term misses of financial objectives. Lengthening the period of time management has to create and report different classes of information allows the firm greater time to glean insights from this information.

Communication both to internal and external end users is imperative for any strategic initiative or change, and integrated reporting certainly represents a paradigm shift for any management team or organization. Effectively managing expectations, setting guidelines, and establishing channels of communication between the organization and, arguably, the most active and engaged stakeholder group cannot be outsourced to one functional area or department. Rather, particularly at the beginning of this process, managing the feedback and input from shareholder groups and other investors enables buy-in from external stakeholder groups and the development of an effective long-term plan. This communication strategy and buy-in is also linked to how integrated reporting is connected to the long-term value creation strategy and ideals espoused by institutional and other long-term investors.

Integrated Reporting and Differentiated Reporting

Information is how decisions are made, and while more information may indeed assist in the decision-making process, it is also certainly possible that the sheer volume of data may be in excess of what certain stakeholders need to assess organizational performance. An important step in the adoption and implementation of integrated reporting, and a data point that will be expanded in more detail (in the implementation section of this text) is the ability of integrated reporting to facilitate more customized and differentiated reporting. Different stakeholders, whether are they are nonfinancial and financial in nature, require, expect, and ultimately use different types of information depending on the industry, size of organization, and opinion of management teams. Something that can be stated with confidence is not every piece of information available at the organization is going to be of interest to every stakeholder group.

One common complaint, even taking into account the variety of information, is that information is only reported at periodic intervals. Linking back to the underlying methodology and goal of integrated reporting is namely the idea that a variety of information can be reported on a more continuous basis. As organizations, via the implementation of different technology tools and platforms inside the company are more able to ascertain the impact of information on external reporting, the ability to customize reports will increase. The end form of said reports, whether it is dashboards, bullet points, summaries, or presentations is less important than the purpose of any information communicated to external stakeholders, namely, to better inform and educate stakeholders to assist in the decision-making process. Traditional financial reporting, even when properly reported and distributed on a timely basis does not add the same amount of information and insight to every stakeholder constituency. Put simply, different end users of financial information require and use different types of information to evaluate choices and the decision-making process.

It is clear that simply implementing a new reporting framework or structure will not address the numerous gaps and needs of stakeholder groups, but it is important to revisit the benefits associated with developing a more comprehensive framework. First, creating a reporting template and framework utilizing many of the same attributes of traditional financial reporting allows external users to more consistently analyze and compare the results of nonfinancial information. Second, linking together the idea of reporting quantitative metrics on a reduced basis, or even on a basis more closely aligned with operational realities, makes more sense when attempting to connect the performance of the organization to the different streams of information already produced by the firm.

Integrated reporting, when specifically embedding the multiple capital model within the framework provides management with the ability to not only organize information internally, but to also quantify and report these types of information to stakeholders. The benefits and implications of a multiple capital model are clearly recognizable for internal decision-making and evaluating different options, but there are also implications for external reporting that should be acknowledged. In addition to the reality that a multiple capital model allows management professionals within an organization to report different flows and varieties of information to internal users, it also allows the customization and creation of action-oriented reports for different end users. Different stakeholder groups, while interested almost universally in the financial performance of the organization, are also interested in different aspects of just how the organization is obtaining these financial results.

For example, and increasingly important in a business environment and business landscape beset with technological innovation, the regulatory landscape, and reporting to a variety of organizations, being able to satisfy, and fulfill the expectations of regulators, including both consistency and transparency, are key. Drilling down specifically into some of the upsides and benefits of an integrated reporting framework, as it pertains to differentiated and customizable reports, there are a few items that should be addressed and asked prior to the development and implementation of different reports for different stakeholders.

Specifically, management teams and associated organizations should be asked to address the following questions:

1. How often do different stakeholders receive information? The frequency with which stakeholder groups receive information will, inevitably, play a role in the

types of information and data expected and utilized by different stakeholder groups. Taking into account this fact, financial stakeholders including both creditors and equity shareholders most likely expect and are accustomed to receiving data on a quarterly and semiannual basis. This may certainly be appropriate in some situations, but in a real-time environment increasingly dominated by technology such periodic updates are insufficient to inform real-time decision-making:

a. Specifically, what are the different nonfinancial factors that can influence the results of the organization in the short, medium and long-term? These include, but are not limited to environmental, regulatory, and legal factors that can change the operational and financial realities of the competitive landscape.

b. Are there different types of information, including the reams of data generated on an ongoing basis that would appear to fit both into the multiple capital model and the interest areas of stakeholders? Specifically, this stage of the conversation should take place between management, financial professional within the organization, and specific stakeholders.

2. What data actually matters to stakeholder groups? It may seem repetitive, but this is a question and perspective that cannot be overstated or reiterated too often; not all information currently distributed by organizations matters to all stakeholder groups. In fact, and a driving force behind the continued adoption of integrated reporting by different organizations, is the reality that many stakeholders do not even understand the financial information currently published and communicated by organizations. This gap may appear to be an abstract issue or idea, but analogies can be utilized to help illustrate the issues that may arise as a result of this miscommunication:

a. For example, if an organization produced a good or service the majority of people did not find useful, would that organization remain in business for very long? The answer is clearly no, and this reality would be the same regardless of what industry, geographic region, or demographic group this organization serves. In an environment increasingly dependent on information, both for internal decision-making and for external stakeholders to evaluate the performance of an organization, disseminating information unhelpful to many stakeholders is a recipe for negative results.

b. Building on this dialogue and having the sometimes-difficult conversations of addressing what data are actually helpful for external users, a facet and value proposition of integrated reporting becomes readily apparent. Different stakeholders, like different organizations and individuals in any other context, often require and refer to different types of information and services to make decisions. The multiple capital model aspect of the integrated reporting provides a quantitative platform for management professionals to build differentiated reporting for end user.

3. Ascertain what types of capital, embedded in the multiple capital model, are realistically most applicable and appropriate for communication to different stakeholder groups given the competitive context of the organization. This analysis and fact-finding mission, however, is not something that can simply be delegated or assigned to some subset of employees—it has to be an organizational priority and prerogative. Clearly different stakeholders are going to be interested in different types of information and data, but five key questions can, and should, be asked when determining what types of data should be communicated and quantified for stakeholder groups:

   a. What are the broader business forces influencing the decisions made by these stakeholder groups?

   b. Does the organization have access to the information necessary to communicate and disseminate different streams of information?

   c. Are there certain business trends, such as environmental or regulatory trends influencing the competitive landscape that management should take into account when developing reporting frameworks?

   d. Is there an ongoing and current conversation and dialogue underway between management and external users of organizational information? Some may assume such a situation exists, but it is important to ensure a constructive dialogue and relationship does exist.

   e. Does the company have the correct and appropriate personnel in place to actually produce this information?

4. Identify and quantify the broader business changes, including but not limited to regulatory and competitive changes that are driving how the organization operates and competes. There is no crystal ball option available, regardless of which reporting template of framework is utilized, so there will always be an element of uncertainty when forecasting or projecting trends. That said, there are several areas of broader business trends and changes that are both important for business performance, and connect directly to the integrated reporting framework:

   a. *Regulatory changes*: In the United States, where several major regulatory matters include but are not limited to trade negotiations, tax reform, and ongoing health care policy it is evident that regulation is currently in flux. Other markets, such as the Asia-Pacific region and Europe, however, are not representative of stability. With uncertainty around a postBrexit European Union, and a somewhat contentious landscape developing between China and regional trading partners, instability and shifting regulation is something everything organization must take into account:

      i. The transparency and increased availability of information generated and communicated by integrated reporting can assist, as organization and regulators both attempt to successfully navigate a fluid business landscape.

b. *Stakeholder transition*: The phrase stakeholders traditionally referred to nonprofit organizations, NGOs, and other nonfinancial stakeholders but this definition is insufficient when trying to implement and sustain integrated reporting. Put simply, and perhaps most recently illustrated by Blackrock, the largest passive asset management firm in the world, financial shareholders and investment professionals are increasingly interested in the long-term performance of organizations:

   i. This is a point and perspective that cannot be overlooked when introducing the concept and idea of integrated reporting to the shareholder community and financial analysts. While there is no sign quarterly earnings will become less important in the near term, linking this shift to a more a comprehensive view of reporting is an important step in the introductory and adoption process.

c. *Competitive landscape*: The 5 forces model has driven with near impunity how organizations and management teams that run them judge both the marketplace and what decisions are made in the competitive landscape. This framework, dynamic and creative in its own right, certainly still delivers value to management team but needs to be updated in light of an increasingly mercurial and multifaceted competitive landscape. Drilling down specifically and connecting these changes to integrated reporting, several items should appear logical to include:

   i. What is the status and positioning of our core business?

   ii. What actually is the core business of our organization, meaning what goods and services do customers and clients seek from our organization?

   iii. What areas of nonfinancial information are most important for our business and management on a continuous basis?

d. Financial pressures and the longer-term view of financial performance is also a factor that connects to the integrated reporting framework. Specifically, how organizations and management teams focus on comprehensive performance, and how the company achieves these financial results. Financial information is already analyzed and examined in a thorough manner, but connecting the short-term financial information and the longer-term success of an organization can be difficult and challenging, even in the most profitable and growth-oriented business environments. In the globally competitive environment every organization currently finds itself in, however, there is additional pressure often brought to bear on management to fulfill quarterly earnings objectives. Simply adopting an integrated reporting homework, in and of itself, will not assist management in making longer-term decisions, but it does provides a platform to communicate information. Specifically, there are several tactics and ideas management teams can use to bridge the gap between what is often analyzed by the marketplace, and what is necessary for sustainable long-term growth.

Integrated Reporting and Long-Term Value Creation

Generating value and achieving returns over the long term is a strategy and idea discussed by numerous shareholder groups, and which should be of interest to virtually every stakeholder audience. Even with the rise in interest and conversation surrounding the benefits of investing for the long term, building a durable and robust strategy in the face of competitive forces is difficult, as there are contradictory forces that can blunt the power of said arguments. Circling back to one of the underlying issues with nonfinancial and stakeholder-based reporting, it is all too easy to lose focus and commitment to the long-term value creation, especially if information is not communicated in a consistent and standardized manner. Integrated reporting, which includes different types of information, creates a template and framework that can be in communication channels. Creating value requires financial investment, the dedication and commitment of personnel, and the ability to successfully engage with stakeholders through bull and bear markets (Figure 6.2).

Value creation is an interesting concept to understand when taking into account the adoption of integrated reporting in a business environment consistently tracking the performance of an organization from a financial basis, and comparing the organization to peers within the same industry. Generating and sustaining value over the long term, which can vary depending on the specific industry, is an important perspective integrated reporting assists in highlighting. Constructing a framework and outline both comparable and understandable can help in connecting the proverbial dots between bottom line performance and the fundamental performance of the organization. While numerous frameworks exist, integrated reporting takes current progress one step further by quantifying these different streams of data into classes of capital.

By developing a framework there is an additional benefit that accrues to management teams and organizations, which might not be initially available, but is equally as important to sustaining the value creation process. Connecting the reporting and information communicated by the organization to both internal and external end users with external third-party frameworks and standards provides

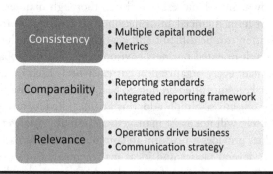

Figure 6.2   The business case for integrated reporting.

additional support and validation. Fortunately, there are numerous options in the market with which integrated reporting can, and should, converge and build on moving forward. Sustainability reporting and disclosures are on the rise, with an overwhelming percentage of organizations reporting and disclosing some level of sustainability data; but simply reporting this information is insufficient, it must be communicated and documented in a quantitative and consistent manner. While different external frameworks exist, there is one framework in particular that appears to be closely linked to integrated reporting and sustainability information: the United Nations Sustainable Development Goals (SDGs).

The United Nations Sustainable Development Goals (SDGs), an extension of the millennium development goals, represent a broad swath of information and data applicable to multinationals operating on a global basis. Since these larger organizations, most of which do operate on a global basis, are the same organizations most likely to adopt integrated reporting, connecting this information to the SDGs is a logical step in the implementation process. While the full scope of the SDGs, which include items like advocating for universal legal frameworks on a global basis, may not apply equally to every organization, the sustainable development aspect of this framework certainly does. Such a connection also reinforces the idea that sustainability and sustainable development does not pertain only to environmentally oriented activities.

Returning to a market perspective on the topic of value creation, which again is critical to sustain the adoption and implementation of any new communication and reporting strategy, organizations can, and should, reference the difference between book value and market value. While clearly a significant portion of this difference is due to historical cost and other fundamental accounting principles, the reality is that a substantial percentage of this difference is attributable to intangible assets. More importantly, especially when engaging with shareholder and stakeholder groups, market valuation (usually higher than the tangible book value of the organization) is also the metric connected to shareholder satisfaction with management and board activities. Market valuation is also a factor cited in comparisons of organizations to different competitors, peers, as well as up and coming new entrants into the competitive landscape. Simply acknowledging this fact, however, neither represents new information nor will assist in establishing the role of integrated reporting moving forward.

The important point to emphasize and play up, rather, is the connection between market valuation, intangible assets, and the importance of communicating the value of these intangibles to both the market at large and specific stakeholder groups. This connection and linkage is not only important for current management teams and professionals, but for emphasizing the validity of integrated reporting activities even during periods of market volatility and economic uncertainty. Financial shareholders are, clearly, most often interested in the most recent results of the organization versus both prior performance and expectations generated by market participants. Integrated reporting provides management with the necessary platform and framework to connect these two concepts, namely the fulfillment of expectations of shareholders and the ability of the organization to sustain financial performance in the medium and longer term.

Sustainable development and business, rather, encompass the broader idea of doing business in a manner that is replicable, consistently achievable, and relevant to the industry. Long-term value creation, which necessitates the organization take action to develop growth prospects in the medium and long term, appears to be in alignment with the concept of sustainable growth and development. By default, in order to achieve growth and profits over the long term, the methods by which this objective is obtained must also reflect a longer-term perspective. Ensuring a common base of understanding between internal management professionals and external stakeholder groups is important, but an important tool to assist with this conversation is the linking of management strategy to externally validated frameworks.

Frameworks are important, regardless of industry or geographic region since they provide a baseline for comparison in terms of both information and the insights generated by different components of an organization. Integrated reporting, by breaking out the different areas of data and information created by organizations in any case, allows management to provide stakeholders with the quantitative information they so often desire.

Building a bridge and connection between the statements of management, actions undertaken by the organization, messaging and optics presented to the market, and connecting the above to existing structures in the market form a comprehensive strategy for the adoption and implementation of integrated reporting. That said, it is not enough to simply link together different areas of an organization to craft a message—quantitative reporting and analysis must also move in lockstep with these changes. Specifically, the accounting function, the implications of technological change, and the connections between management accounting, existing reports, and financial reporting is a logical place to also analyze the implications of integrated reporting moving forward.

Chapter 7

Accounting Implications for Integrated Reporting

As stated both at the beginning of this text and reinforced by way of the different analyses introduced throughout this book, accounting information and data form the lifeblood of business and is the language through which organizations and management professionals are evaluated. That said, and reflecting the changing nature of the profession at large, accounting professionals, including those employed both within organizations and those working in a consultative capacity, must be included in the conversations and change management projects aligned with integrated reporting. Accounting practitioners, already versed and trained in quantifying, reporting, and explaining different types of information and data are uniquely well positioned to facilitate both internal and external conversations connected to integrated reporting. Taking these different forces, including blockchain and artificial intelligence, and connecting them to the overall shift and evolution of how organizational data are reported is important in fully understanding and realizing the benefits of an integrated report and its associated implementation.

Assurance and Attestation Changes

Circling back to prior points made during earlier components of this research, the accounting function and practitioners must evolve and adapt alongside other functional areas within the organization. Framed in a traditional sense and taking into account both the responsibilities of internal management accountants and external professionals advising an organization in an assurance capacity, accounting has trended toward focusing on a handful of factors. First, accounting reports and analysis have traditionally focused on a historical analysis of what has previously occurred at the organization, and been involved in ensuring that this information is reported accurately and consistently. Core concepts and components of accounting information include that this information must be reported on a consistent, timely, relevant, and comparable basis. Clearly these are important elements in any type of information that is either communicated to external users or used to judge and evaluate decisions made internally.

One of the largest changes already looming and having an influence on the profession is the change coming to how attestation and other assurance work is performed by practitioners. While traditional financial and operational information connected to how the organization is performing has developed a thorough and comprehensive framework for analysis and interpretation, other types of data and information continue to evolve. Specifically, the areas of sustainability, operational data, and other traditionally qualitative information, which are also critical parts of integrated financial reporting, represent opportunities for development and refinement of reporting standards. Even more interestingly—taking the perspective of external accounting and auditing firms for a moment, are the revenue and other growth opportunities embedded within these changes and developments.

In addition to the needs of management seeking to improve and clarify current decisions and options, there are also revenue opportunities and potential embedded in the growing need for different types of information from the marketplace. Specifically, as organizations and management teams under pressure from both activist investors, retail shareholders, and institutional partners seek to operate in a more comprehensive manner, accounting firms should take advantage of these opportunities. In addition to increasing revenue in the current marketplace, through engaging assurance and attestation activities with clients, these are future-driven concerns that accounting professionals should take into consideration. If, for example, a CPA practitioner and/or firm desires to sell their firm to other firms in the marketplace, the firm must be able to generate revenues after the initial sale and transition. Making this connection, both at the level of professional associations and individual firms can illustrate some of the potential accompanying this shift.

Sustainability, issuing different types of reports and information for a variety of external stakeholders, and making sure these types of information are valid and accurate are not trends that represent a short-term fad. Rather, trends and information represented by this increased interest in sustainability are linked to both increased amounts of stakeholder interest in these issues and the interest of millennials in the workforce. Stakeholder groups, including financial and nonfinancial stakeholders and institutional groups are interested in both the financial and the nonfinancial implications of sustainability and sustainability reporting. In order to attract millennial employees, retain said employees, and develop a market position appropriate for customers and consumers, accounting professionals must evolve and adopt to this generational shift and change.

While it is true that as the broader business landscape changes the accounting profession will have to change alongside clients and industry actors, there must also be standards, frameworks, and guidance to assist professionals with this transition. The accounting profession is already juggling a variety of changes and regulatory updates, including but not limited to changes in revenue recognition, the shift of all leases being reported on a balance sheet versus some reported in an off balance sheet manner, and changes to how not-for-profit (NFP) organizations report financial results. Stated simply, if organizations want to implement and adopt an integrated reporting framework the management leadership of the firm must be able to quantify, articulate, and demonstrate a valid business case for doing so in the current environment. This information, embedded in the very nature of the multiple capital model, allows organizations to report and disseminate the variety and volume of information required to make effective decision-making in a stakeholder business environment. That said, it is also important for management teams to be able to highlight the opportunities for CPAs and other accounting professionals to expand and elevate work performed by organizations.

Specifically, helping to develop and maintain new methods of assurance services and attestation reports are the direct connections between accounting, integrated reporting, and how the profession must elevate to maintain market position. This mirrors a growing interest in the profession to evolve beyond merely being record keeping and compliance professionals to being more strategic decision makers and business partners. Expectations have also evolved and will continue to evolve as integrated reporting becomes increasingly mainstream and adopted on a global basis. Whether operating as accounting professionals employed within industry or those working in a public practice setting, there are numerous implications that must be considered for moving forward. Put simply, and in addition to the desire of stakeholders to make improved decisions, the expectations of internal and external users have evolved and changed as business becomes increasingly global and digital in nature.

Use Case

The accounting profession continues to evolve and change as the marketplace continues to transform into one almost entirely driven by digitization, globalization, and the connection between nonfinancial information, organizational performance, and the strategic planning process at companies. Numerous changes are already having a dramatic effect on how accounting functions are performed and reported across organizational lines, and this list continues to grow annually. Alterations to revenue recognition, changes to how lease obligations must be reported, and the implications associated with tax reform that will continue to reverberate throughout the landscape are just a handful of these business items changing the landscape. As if these changes were not enough to contend with in an increasingly competitive business environment, there are other powerful forces at work disrupting the profession.

Blockchain technology, artificial intelligence, and the growing automation of how business decisions are made present both an opportunity and a challenge to both management teams and accounting professionals at large. Automation represents a tremendous benefit for organizations seeking to contend with the ever-larger amounts of information generated and reported by the organization. Lower level tasks, verification of data accuracy, and confirming that amounts listed and reported are correct represent time consuming activities, which do not actively add value to the organizational process. These tasks, automated via technology and technology systems, allow management accounting professionals to focus on high-level tasks, coordinating with management to connect raw data to strategic planning, and communicating these initiatives to the marketplace.

Changing Expectations

The true value added proposition of an accounting function is to deliver information that enables decision makers and users of information to make effective, timely, and relevant decisions. While traditional financial information clearly drives different types of decision-making and enables management professionals to view and evaluate the success or failure of different initiatives, a wider variety of information is necessary. Specifically, in a marketplace driven and governed by an increasingly diverse combination of stakeholders and end users, accounting functions and practitioners must be able to deliver the types of information required for effective decision-making. In addition to the different types of information and data necessary to manage and grow the organization over the medium and long term, the ability of accountants to provide information in a continuous and real time manner is a critical component of organizational success.

Real-time information, advisory services, and expertise are not traditionally associated with the accounting profession or practitioners, but represents areas accounting must grow into to deliver value moving forward. Leveraging different types of information technology tools will enable accounting professionals to provide insights required by investors. Generating this real-time information, however, necessitates a new and more holistic platform for reporting information, and integrated reporting appears to offer a solution to the existing mismatch between what accounting professionals provide and what stakeholders expect and require from organizations.

Nonfinancial information does not normally fall under the purview of accounting professionals, nor is it a competency traditionally embedded within the accounting profession. This reinforces the perspective that, in a globalized and increasingly stakeholder-oriented business environment, it is important both financial and nonfinancial information form the basis for strategy and strategic decision-making. Integrated reporting, virtually by default, represents a convergence of both financial and nonfinancial information important for the adoption and implementation of a more comprehensive reporting framework. Applying similar rigor and analyses to nonfinancial data and information is imperative in a business landscape now requiring organizations to report, analyze, and document their success in a variety of ways. Quantifying data, forming reports and dashboards understandable for nonfinancial experts forms a method by which accountants can deliver value to the market at large.

In accounting and accounting information there are several trends and topics that initially come to mind. Specifically, concerning how accounting and accounting information are perceived, the characteristics of accounting information delivering value in the present are the same characteristics that will hamstring the profession moving forward. Accounting data and information, including the reports generated by accounting practitioners, are almost always focused on financial data and are applicable to creditors and shareholders while only reporting information and events that have already occurred. While this certainly does provide value to the stakeholders who are involved in the reporting and data processing process, the action-oriented value based on these reports is limited. Put simply, the information generated by traditional accounting function and practitioner groups do not address the needs, expectations, and requirements of different stakeholder groups.

While different stakeholder groups expect and require information that is prepared in a real manner, provides advice and guidance on a forward-looking basis, and is both available and comparable, the current status and capacity of information provided by accounting professionals does not fulfill these expectations. Accounting data, historical in nature and applicable to a rather narrow set of stakeholders, clearly does not generate the insights and information necessary for management professionals seeking to compete and succeed in a globalized business landscape. These changes already underway in the marketplace, including but not limited to blockchain, artificial intelligence, and advanced analytical tools, and they are creating an environment suited for a more proactive and forward-looking accounting function. Putting into place these systems and integrated reporting processes will, of course, require investments, changes, and upgrades to current accounting systems and processes.

To create a more forward-looking accounting function, however, there are several characteristics and types of information that must be integrated together in the decision-making process. Accounting professionals should, in an integrated reporting environment and landscape, be able to advise management professionals and external stakeholder groups with information that is relevant in a real time-manner, and which has implications for decisions made in the current business landscape. Blockchain in particular has numerous opportunities and options for the accounting profession, as the stakeholder business landscape continues to evolve and develop moving forward. The application of smart contracts in the business environment can generate and create a business environment where accounting information and practitioners can begin providing real-time advice and guidance to management and different stakeholder groups. Drilling down into the different applications and permutations of this technology and platform, there are a few things that accounting and accounting professionals should understand. Blockchain technology is comprised of both a block and chain, forming the immutable record that underpins the fundamental basis of the technology and platform. Taking into account the reality that different industries and realities will apply different technology tools at different rates, it is also important to recognize that integrated reporting is not simply another reporting and compliance requirement. In addition to the informational and reporting context of integrated reporting, it is also worthwhile to examine and analyze the linkage between integrated reporting and additional revenue opportunities.

Chapter 8

Integrated Reporting and Revenue Opportunities

Integrated reporting, although representing a reporting and information communication framework, is much more than simply another compliance-based or oriented activity. Especially important in a business environment already populated by a variety of compliance, regulatory, and other reporting mandates, it is essential that integrated reporting be presented on a holistic basis. What this means for management professionals seeking to lead the adoption of integrated reporting is that it is important to emphasize not only the reporting aspect of integrated financial reporting, but to also emphasize the importance of extended revenue opportunities embedded with the more comprehensive analyzing or reporting of organizational information. Integrated reporting is neither a standalone event or idea, nor does it appear to represent a short-term event or fad, but rather a wholesale change in how organizations collect, report, and analyze information. Connecting this reporting framework to not only this broader change, but also to the opportunities created therein should be an important aspect of any conversation around integrated reporting implementation.

As has been demonstrated throughout this text, the development and implementation of integrated reporting is not a one-time event or something occurring in a vacuum without other external forces influencing the conversation. The reporting and communication of different types of information is something that forms the basis of how management professionals make decisions, deal with stakeholder requests and questions, and weave the narrative to support the strategic initiatives underway in an organization. That said, reporting information to both internal and external stakeholder groups is not the only aspect of integrated reporting of interest to professional user groups. In addition to the enhanced and more comprehensive information generated and reported by organization marketplace actors, the rise of integrated reporting also creates revenue opportunities. Sustainability, integrated reporting, and the intersection of operational and financial information is connected to broader trends and changes in sustainability and sustainability opportunities.

Specifically, connecting together the trend of integrated reporting and the rising interest in sustainability by a variety of end-user groups, the possibility of new revenue opportunities is apparent. While communicating the initiatives and projects linked to sustainability is clearly important for NGOs, environmental groups, and institutional shareholders, it also allows management to participate in new revenue generating opportunities. Focusing the attention of management on the information streams created by sustainability projects and initiatives, both operational and financial in nature, also allows management's team to observe and plan future initiatives. For example, if after installing an increased numbers of sensors and reporting platforms within the organization to facilitate the reporting process, management becomes aware of additional opportunities for efficiency improvement, they will have the information necessary to make the necessary decisions. Examples of sustainability projects and initiatives abound in the marketplace, indicating that this increased interest in sustainability is not merely an academic discussion. Linking together the increased frequency of sustainability reporting, the implementation of integrated reporting on a global scale, and the growing number of sustainability linked businesses, an underlying trend becomes clear.

Integrated reporting requires management to focus on sustainability information at the same level as financial and other operational information. Examples of sustainability operations and business lines are present in the marketplace and include some of the following examples. General Electric, a large multinational organization with operations that span different geographic areas and industry lines is an almost ideal example of an organization that has utilized the increased digitization of information and connections to achieve sustainability. Ecomagination, the business division established by the management team during the financial crisis in 2008 has generated in excess of $100 billion of revenues since its inception. Granted, General Electric represents an organization that certainly has access to the necessary resources and personnel to implemented such an ambitious plan, but the success of this business division highlights the intersection of business management, improved analytics, and sustainability initiatives.

Clearly one successful business segment does not a trend make, but such a high profile example is interesting for a number of reasons. First, the trend toward increased disclosure and reporting of sustainability data and information has been evolving and growing in the face of market and stakeholder expectations. With trillions of dollars invested toward sustainability initiatives, and numerous market indices oriented around environmental, social, and governance investing strategies, the appetite and desire for this information is readily apparent. In addition to the financial capital allocated toward these objectives, the external stakeholder environment has evolved alongside the sustainability continuum. Whether it takes the form of differentiated governmental regulation, institutional pressure brought to bear by the largest investors, or shifting consumer tastes the stakeholder environment has evolved alongside the reporting landscape.

It is also important to acknowledge that integrated reporting is not a process or event that will happen instantaneously or on a onetime basis. Additionally, the implementation process of integrated reporting will, inevitably, unveil and reveal operational gaps, shortcomings, and additional opportunities for business development and growth during the implementation process. While perhaps not readily apparent upon initial examination, the connection between advanced analytics, management insights, and integrated reporting is a logical one. In order to successfully implement integrated reporting, it is important to remember that management professionals must have access to the data and information necessary to generate reports and data consistent with a multiple capital model. As previously discussed, the necessary changes to internal processes and systems to facilitate this reporting process requires that the organization confront internal silos and other stumbling blocks to the flow of information.

Taking a step back and reflecting once again on the success of organizations such as Southwest, there does appear to be some connection between successful organizations, a sustainability mindset, and (at this point at least) the implementation of integrated reporting. Creating new revenue opportunities and business markets certainty falls under the purview of management's responsibility and fiduciary duty; and while integrated reporting itself may not generate revenue, the insights produced may do just that. Linking together the data produced by the organization, various initiatives and programs put into place by the management team, and the financial impact of said plans also provide a fertile ground for future work and implementation. Perhaps the most clear-cut example of such a connection would be a situation where, upon making some incremental changes to data collection and reporting processes, management discovers internal opportunities to reduce costs and improve efficiency. In addition to generating a positive connection between integrated reporting implementation and financial results—of interest to both financial and nonfinancial stakeholders—the positive momentum can be applied moving forward. Building on this earlier success, internal proponents and supporters of integrated reporting can apply these insights to other business divisions and segments.

Akin to the approach taken by Adidas, where insights and strategies generated as a result of sustainability investments are applied across global business lines, the information and data created through this enhanced transparency can benefit the entire organization. Drilling down specifically, it is also important to keep in mind that in addition to increased insights and visibility into internal operation and those associated benefits, this increased information may also form the basis of competitive advantages moving forward. In a business environment increasingly digital in nature, the management professionals and organizations that are best able to leverage data would appear to gain a substantial advantage in the marketplace. Building on initial insights, most likely related to internal efficiency gains, opens the door to further initiatives and projects constructed on the platform of increased information availability as a result of integrated reporting.

Connecting Integrated Reporting to Talent Development

The idea of human capital is already embedded into the integrated reporting framework via the multiple capital framework, but this connection spans a broader category of decisions matrix than even just reporting information. Human capital, summarized and highlighted by the tracking and reporting of talent development, training, and employee training appears to be a logical place to begin this conversation. Building on this platform, another way to connect the possibly abstract idea of human capital to operational decisions is to emphasize cost savings and efficiencies generated through lower employee turnover. These benefits and connections are, in virtually every instance, benefits and upsides already recognized in the marketplace, however an underlying trend may have gone overlooked. This trend connects both the ability of an organization to effectively report success and succeed in the marketplace, and the capability to grow and compete moving forward, is the ability of the organization to attract and retain top quality talent. Millennials, already assuming positions of leadership on a global scale, and in some cases even occupying the positions of heads of state, will continue to have a powerful impact on the marketplace for years to come.

At a high level, and being careful not overly to utilize generalizations—never entirely accurate—there appear to be several trends and factors specific to this generation that connect to the growing interest in integrated reporting. First, on average and from all available market evidence, millennials are more likely to want to work for a company that either makes a difference and/or enables employees to make a difference. In addition to possibly reflecting echoes of the financial crisis, this represents a definitive connection between increasing stakeholder interest and the interest of employees who will be managing these organizations. Technology tools, including automation and artificial intelligence, will continue to drive decision-making, but the outlook of employees using these tools cannot be overlooked. Second, millennials are more likely on average to want to work for organizations involved in their broader stakeholder communities, which also forms the basis of stakeholder pressure emerging from traditional financial investors.

Building bridges to the broader community may, at first glance, appear more like nonfinancial appeal to aspects of the business landscape not usually associated with generating returns. Taking a step back, however, and realizing that nothing exists in a vacuum—including organizations, creates a lens through which these initiatives can be viewed constructively. For example, and highlighted by the efforts focusing on water stewardship currently underway at Coca-Cola, there are direct business benefits to being an engaged member of the stakeholder community. Other initiatives may include providing seed capital, capital equipment, or expertise for job training opportunities. This creates a virtuous cycle of broader engagement, a better trained and positioned work force, and an organization that benefits (in the form of hiring these employees) from this investment. With skill set mismatches routinely cited as an organizational challenge across industry lines, creating an environment where the skills learned are the skills needed simply makes good business sense.

Last but not least, and important to remember when taking account of business management in a globalized business environment, is that the millennial generation and potential employee base is not limited to one country, area, or demographic group. As this subset of the population continues to obtain education, assets, and become a more pronounced voice in the global conversation this trend will only increase. Stakeholder engagement, sustainability efforts and initiatives, and connecting with the broader trend toward stakeholder management represent definitive influential business trends. Millennial employees and members of the community will only accentuate these developments.

Integrated Reporting and External Opportunities

On top of the benefits and insights linked to generating internal management decision-making, it is important to also link back to opportunities for external advisory and consulting organizations. Mentioned previously, stakeholder interest in sustainability, sustainability reporting, and the importance of sustainable operations is only positioned to grow and move forward. Accounting and other quantitatively oriented organizations, for example, are well positioned to report, analyze, and explain the potential and insights driven by increased access to information within organizations. Existing competencies and skills embedded within the accounting profession include the quantitative analysis of information, explaining a narrative to highlight important insights derived from said information, and reporting data in an understandable format. Such competencies and skills also converge with outputs and data generated as a result of integrated reporting implementation.

While the connection between integrated reporting, benefits and insights as applied to internal management, and the applications for accounting professionals may seem tenuous, upon further analysis a stronger connection emerges. In order to both convince the market of the validity of integrated reported, as well as the insights contained therein, there must be more consistent analysis of just what the implications of integrated reporting mean for organizations. Creating an environment where the multiple classes of capital are reported and classified on a consistent and replicable manner is an essential first step toward establishing a baseline for further acceptance of integrated reporting by stakeholder groups. Lending this expertise and background in reporting information, and quantifying different streams and varieties of information provides both an opportunity and challenge for external accounting professionals.

Taking this perspective into account also reveals another important aspect of integrated reporting to remember and keep in mind when considering adoption in the context of broader business performance. Business decisions are almost exclusively driven or at least supported by the quantitative information produced and communicated by an organization, so it is logical that as more information and data become available for management analysis, more and different revenue opportunities will inevitably come online for business utilization. Developing new business segments, product lines, service opportunities, and market penetration strategies are often considered to represent the proverbial secret sauce for sustainable business growth. Harnessing the increased variety and types of information developed and available via an integrated reporting framework is a logical first step in this process.

As the information and insights created via integrated reporting implementation and adoption by organizations become more widespread and accepted by external end users, the importance of accounting professionals in the conversations will continue to grow. Let us not forget that at the core of the concept and idea of integrated reporting, and other nonfinancial reporting platforms, lies the will to establish parity between short-term financial and other longer-term financial information. Developing standards and reporting templates, with coordination between organizations and external consultative experts, will assist in this process. Put simply, in order for nonfinancial information to achieve an appropriate level of acceptance, external professionals in the accounting financial industries must become part of the conversation and dialogue. It is also important to integrate into any current and projected analysis of integrated financial reporting that there is an embedded value proposition in this framework. While the framework itself is, at the end of the day, a reporting and communication framework, it is also connected to broader trends in the economy and marketplace. Connecting these various forces, building these bridges, and communicating this to internal and external users help to validate, reinforce, and illustrate the core value propositions of integrated reporting.

Chapter 9

The Value Proposition of Integrated Reporting

At the end of the day, any additional work or initiative launched by an organization should be connected to not only improving the quality of information communicated by the organization, but also increasing the value created by the organization for both internal and external stakeholder groups. The core value of integrated reporting can, and should be, connected to increases in operational efficiency, market capitalization, and returns generated from a financial perspective for the organization. It is important to remember and continuously circle back to the underlying concept of integrated reporting when constructing the value model for implementation. First, improved data communication and dissemination allows management teams to potentially head off activist investors or other distractions before they become full-fledged distractions for the management team. Second, increasing the amount of focus and attention invested in analyzing and reporting other types of information, on top of and in addition to financial data, creates an environment in which additional insights can be turned into action-oriented business insights. Last, by harnessing the power of operational data, as this chapter explains, management and employees throughout the organization now have the ability to make effective business decisions for the organization as a whole, and not just with financial stakeholders in mind.

At the end of 2017, there were hundreds of organizations issuing an integrated report as per the IIRC database, with many of these organizations highlighted as quality examples of said reporting. As with many other trends, including technology, blockchain, and artificial intelligence, the adoption and implementation curve of integrated reporting has begun with the larger and multinational organizations. While this is partly a function of these larger organizations in terms of resources and personnel, it also reflects the reality that larger companies have the complexity embedded in operations to require this enhanced transparency and disclosure. Taking a broader perspective, and looking over the breadth of the economy on a holistic basis, it appears clear that integrated reporting epitomizes the convergence of several broader trends and forces in the marketplace. Looking at these various other options serves two distinct purposes.

First, while alternate frameworks may be, in essence, competing with the integrated reporting framework, the validity and rigor involved in the creation of alternative frameworks signals a growing interest in these associated areas. While alternative proponents of various frameworks and methodologies may differ on specific approaches, recommendations, and methods of communication the underling focus and drive is similar. Specifically, the SASB frameworks and recommendations are performed on an industry-by-industry basis, and are oriented specifically toward SEC implementation. This approach certainly has significant merit, and has created a dynamic conversation and dialogue around how to quantify and report sustainability information to the marketplace. One distinction between the SASB reporting and the idea of integrated financial reporting is that while the SASB tends to focus on sustainability information, integrated reporting focuses on creating a comprehensive view of organizational performance. One area both frameworks share, despite other differences and variations is the idea of an increasingly circular and environmentally oriented economy.

Creating Value in the Marketplace

Generating value for shareholders and stakeholders is clearly a fiduciary duty and responsibility of management regardless of industry lines, but this duty can all too often overshadow the importance of creating value over the medium and long term. Especially in a business environment and landscape increasingly dominated by technology, intellectual assets, and intangible value generators this is no longer a conversation that can be considered optional in nature. Rather, as stakeholder and shareholder interest in the intangible assets and intellectual capital of an organization grow more pronounced, management has a responsibility to fulfill these expectations. Quantifying a specific pattern and pathway to do so, however, has been difficult in the past and can result in inconsistent progress, lack of robust reporting frameworks, and a mindset that such activities are more related to public relations than operational decisions. Using a metric such as market valuation, already used by financial professionals internal and external to the organization, can help create a dialogue productive and forward-looking in nature. There is a danger, however, that by emphasizing market valuation and other external indicators (or company worth) many of the same issues currently plaguing management, including short-termism, will only be accentuated. Framed in that context, the value of an integrated reporting framework becomes even more apparent.

Integrated reporting, at the core of the concept, emphasizes the idea of long-term value creation both sustainable in terms of its impact on the environment and the ability of organizations to generate these results over the longer term. The connection between value creation and market capitalization can appear to be exclusively oriented toward the short-term activities all too common at larger organizations, but that does not have to be the case. Organizations such as Amazon and Tesla, for example, even as both firms operate in capital intensive industries with extensive competition, have been able to generate value for shareholders, delight customers, and do so on a continuous basis. Other more established organizations may have struggled after introducing sustainability initiatives, such as General Electric, and this is important for two reasons. First, integrated reporting—or any other reporting framework for that matter, is not a panacea or magic solution to issues plaguing the market; competition and business cycles are an inevitable part of the business cycle. Second, even if an organization attempts to more comprehensively integrate sustainability into business operations, this is not a guarantee that those specific business activities will result in benefits to ongoing business activities.

By connecting the operations of the organization, changes to market valuation, and engagement with stakeholder groups, management professionals are provided with a metric and roadmap to successfully connect strategic initiatives to investments. Additionally, while the investments may not currently have an accretive effect on earnings in the current period, the relationship between investments, current results, and strategic operations is possible.

Circular Economy

The concept of a circular economy, at the essence of the idea, is that organizations and other stakeholder groups must operate in a manner that generates value in the short, medium, and long term. While this concept is not necessarily a new concept or idea, the methods by which organizations achieve these goals and objectives can vary from organization to organization. One common thread underpinning this initiative, however, is the reality that organizations should recycle, reinvest, and attempt to make the most of existing resources via operations. Such an approach clearly appeals to more environmentally conscious stakeholder groups, but is also attracting the attention of traditional investing and investor groups. Drilling down specifically, the implications of operating in a more circular and comprehensive manner for an organization operating in a global business environment are clear. First, and not insignificant in nature, is the reality that as global corporations become more ubiquitous in the lives of consumers, profiles and scrutiny rise accordingly. High profile examples of corporate malfeasance continue to highlight failures and gaps in how organizations operate; and consumers increasingly take notice.

Social media may indeed represent the specific platform by which data and different flows of information are communicated and disseminated from the organization to a host of end users, but the idea of a circular economy applies both internally and externally to the organization in question. It is important to examine and connect, once again, how the idea and concept of a circular economy applies to both a financial and operational structure to facilitate the integration of the circular economy concept with the current business information. Financial implications of operating in a more sustainable and environmentally savvy manner have been documented in numerous articles and other media venues, but bridging the gap between this coverage and the concept of a more circular economy is something integrated reporting can assist with facilitating.

Fueled by social media, the hundreds of millions of global millennials with an ever-increasing amount of purchasing power continue to influence organization behaviors, product lines, and initiatives launched. Second, cost savings and efficiencies linked to managing an organization in a circular and environmentally sensitive manner are not items that can simply be labeled as headline matters. Whether it is driven by firms like Coca-Cola and Adidas launching comprehensive programs internally, organizations like General Electric that have constructed an entire business segment focused on linking sustainability to analytics and data management, or a disruptor such as Tesla that has caused changes throughout an entire industry on a global basis, the underlying trend is apparent. Put simply, management professionals, even those with a long-term orientation, would not operate in certain ways unless there existed quantitative proof that said activities benefit organizations. This undeniable fact also connects to a trend that is both broader in nature, but increasing across industry lines.

Human Capital and Long-Term Value Creation

Much has been written about the importance of human capital, employee development and training, and the connection between human capital and long-term value creation. Not only do the concepts of sustainability, sustainable operations, and employee development improve employee morale, attract, and retain employees, it also connects to the increased importance of intangible assets. Intangible assets, in terms of share of market value for publicly traded organizations and companies, have increased from a minimal to much larger percentage and are increasingly occupying increased amounts of time. While the specifics of intangible assets will vary from organization to organization, the underlying importance of data, intangible assets, and other sorts of nonphysical assets are increasing in value. Intellectual property, such as for organizations like Amazon, Google, and Tesla clearly form the basis for competitive advantages when competing both domestically and internationally. In a not such a strange coincidence, organizations that are most invested in digital assets and intellectual property also appear to represent market leaders and dominant forces in the industries they compete within.

Employee training and development, usually associated with human resources or treated as an ancillary item to core business operations, is arguably more important than previously with the rapid pace of changes in the business landscape. Advances in technology that include, but are not limited to blockchain technology, artificial intelligence, and advanced analytical tools require that management professionals, organizations as a whole, and employees at every level become better equipped with technology options and tools. Employees, all too often, are treated and reported as an expense on the organizational financial statements, and while this may be technically correct from a technical accounting perspective, it shortchanges the long-term benefits of engagement, training, and employee development. Connecting these two forces, namely the initiatives underway at organizations across industry lines and the requirements for management professionals to comply with accounting requirements, requires a more robust reporting structure and communication methodology. Integrated reporting, while clearly not a cure-all for issues and maladies impacting organizations and management decision-making, does appear to provide a path forward.

Better Data for Better Decision-Making

In order to make effective decisions in any business landscape, especially in a global landscape increasingly influenced by the digitization of streams of information, data are imperative for management decision-making. This is not a revolutionary new idea or concept, but the nature of the data necessary for effective decision-making in a stakeholder environment is certainly evolving and changing. Financial information and metrics may represent the end result of data currently evaluated and judged by analysts and market participants, but these results are generated by operational and other organizational activities. Specifically, information derived from customer engagements, supplier interactions, and feedback from both the market and regulators can, and often do, form the basis for management activities. The ability to receive and understand these different streams of information data in a real-time and continuous manner appears to represent a competitive advantage for management professionals and organizations moving forward.

In order to make decisions that are both timely and relevant in nature for an organization, as well as the individual projects, embedded management team must be equipped with appropriate levels of information to evaluate options.

The integrated reporting framework, by its very nature of incorporating a wider array and variety of information into reporting and communication frameworks, represents a quantitative step toward such comprehensive integration of information. Sustainability data, operational results and information, training and employee development, and the integration of strategic information and planning into the decision-making process make significant differences as to just how information and strategy is communicated and executed. Any management professional, team, or organization, will inevitably cite increased information and analytical capability as a decided benefit and upside of technology integration. Looking forward, however, it will be important for organizations to adapt and change to the technological landscape and not remain stagnant. While the specific platforms and tools may evolve and change over time, drilling into several of the current trends appears to be a logical place to begin this analysis.

Chapter 10

Connecting Integrated Reporting to Technology Trends

As has been emphasized throughout this text, the implementation and successful adoption of integrated reporting will require the utilization of technology tools to facilitate the automation and digitization of information. While it is clear that technology, in and of itself, will not successfully lead to the adoption and implementation of integrated reporting, technology tools will assist with automating information to allow enhanced decision-making. The core connection and bridge between integrated reporting and emerging technology tools is that these two concepts and forces have emerged virtually simultaneously in the broader business landscape, and should be reflected as such in the accounting conversation both for practitioners working in industry, as well as those employed in a public practice perspective. It is important to take into account the impact these potentially revolutionary technologies will have on the business landscape. Enhanced reporting and a better analysis and comprehension of information are important not only in the short term, but also in the medium to longer term. Put simply, blockchain and AI represent paradigm shifts within both the profession and how external users receive and interpret organizational information. Taking full advantage of the power and scope of these technology tools is a responsibility of both management professionals employed at the organization, and the technology experts tasked with implementing solutions in this area.

As discussed previously, the implementation and adoption of integrated reporting is not driven purely by technology tools, but technology trends and platforms will drive the specifics of how integrated reporting is implemented at a variety of

149

organizations. The individual product names, specific platforms, and individual firms providing technology tools and services will inevitably change and experience disruptions due to market forces, but three trends do appear to be emerging. Trends and forces such as these appear to be changing not only how organizations do business internally, but also how the management professionals at said organizations interact with different stakeholder groups. Circling back to the integration of technology and reporting trends and the importance of human capital in a stakeholder-oriented environment, the linkage between technology and improved reporting becomes readily apparent. Examining the high-level trends and forces influencing the accounting and finance profession and the reporting process within organizations, three trends emerge as especially prominent. Artificial intelligence, blockchain, and the increased integration of analytics into business decision-making represent forces and technology platforms generating a paradigm shift in the business environment. Examining these forces and trends provides and illustrative framework to connect technology to changes in the reporting environment.

Integrated Reporting: Technology Driven Communication

While it is important for organizations to leverage technology, including the topics we are going to discuss in more detail below, to create and communicate a more comprehensive framework, it is also important to remember that integrated reporting is a communication tool. Organizations are already reporting financial information to the marketplace at an ever-increasing pace, including financial results linked to short-term results as well as longer-term information. Analysts, larger institutional shareholders, and the market at large are used to digesting certain types of information distributed on a certain timeline. Changing this methodology, pace, and content of communication requires management professionals to harness technology tools to facilitate this transition. Artificial intelligence, blockchain, and even cryptocurrencies are positioned to have a disruptive effect on the types and frequency of information communication from organizations to end users. Prior to drilling down in more detail, however, it is important to recognize the reality that integrated reporting serves two primary purposes, as currently constituted and interpreted by market participants:

1. Improved decision-making for the medium and long term by weaving and connecting different types of information into how internal decisions are evaluated, executed, and sustained over the life of the initiative; and
2. A more continuous and transparent method of communicating and engaging with stakeholder groups to enable a more productive and constructive dialogue over the future of the organization and the direction of investments moving forward.

Artificial Intelligence

Working definition: Artificial intelligence, for the purposes of this conversation and general understanding, is not an abstract or terribly complicated topic to understand. In short, the idea of artificial intelligence is that it represents computer programs and software protocols enabling computer systems to make decisions that previously required human oversight and review.

While the topic of artificial intelligence may generate different interpretations and feedbacks depending on the industry, the underlying reality and implications of artificial intelligence are apparent across industry lines. In essence, what advances in artificial intelligence platforms allow management professionals to do is, in effect, to delegate and outsource some of the lower level data analysis and entry functions previously assigned to employees. At first glance this may seem like a trend and implication that merely reduces the probability for employment at entry levels, but this represents an incomplete view of what artificial intelligence means for organizations and employees at all levels. Perhaps the most direct connection between integrated reporting and advances in artificial intelligence is connected to the increased availability of information and data for decision-making.

Whether manifested by the Internet of things (IoT), smart sensors, or increased feedback and information from consumers and other stakeholder groups, the trend toward information availability increases is readily apparent. As a greater and wider variety of information is generated and collected by organizations, a logical follow-up is to attempt to quantify and report this information to internal and external users. With the sheer volume of data and information generated, simply through continuing and ongoing operations, it is in the interest of financial and nonfinancial stakeholders to present, analyze, and report data in a consistent format. Especially important, and linking back to the integrated reporting framework is that many of these streams of information are nonfinancial in nature, but may have a dramatic effect on the financial performance of the organization. Artificial intelligence platforms and tools, regardless of the specific tool or platform utilized by organizations, provide management teams with the ability to make more effective decisions on a continuous basis.

For example, artificial intelligence allows the organization to not only analyze information present in the company and generated by operations, but to clean and clarify the information prior to applying it to decision-making opportunities. Simply obtaining and collecting information generated from operations and other activities underway at the organization is insufficient in a stakeholder-oriented environment. To fully implement integrated reporting, or any other types of advanced reporting and disclosure protocols, management professionals must be able to rely on both the quality and quantity of information. Improving the quality of organizational information is an initial step toward creating and reporting the information contained within the multiple capital model. Implementing artificial intelligence tools will not, obviously, solve any issues or problems at the organization in terms of communication issues but will facilitate the processing of data in a more streamlined manner.

Integrated reporting, as well as the benefits and costs associated with implementing such a program, requires that information be both available to management professionals and presented in a manner comparable and understandable to external end users. Obtaining and having access to different streams of data and information is insufficient, the information must also be prepared and presented in an efficient and clear-cut manner. Even with the increased volume of data at the proverbial fingertips of management professionals, tools and protocols are necessary to clean, coordinate, and repot information in a consistent and comparable manner. In addition to cleaning and presenting the massive amounts of information and data, artificial intelligence also frees up the time for employees to participate in the higher level activities necessary to formulate and communicate the strategic planning process. Information in and of itself, no matter the volume aligned and generated by the organization, cannot simply be generated and communicated. With the growing occurrence of hacks, data breaches, and corporations losing access and control over their information, security over information and data is increasingly important. Fortunately, there is an additional trend and force gaining wider acceptance, which may address this information and data generated by various organizations.

Why it Matters

Artificial intelligence may seem like an idea or concept that is far off into the future, or a concept not directly connected to the financial reporting of an organization. But such an approach and view is not only incorrect, but potentially leaves organizations open to disruption by more innovative competitors. Artificial intelligence is a technology like any other tool, and while initial implementation may be clustered in certain technology organizations and among some of the largest multinational firms in the marketplace, the potential of this platform appears to be only just emerging. A common question or concern with regards to artificial intelligence in the reporting environment is that many organizations and the professionals who run these firms are unsure where to begin. This topic and area can appear intimidating, but it does not have to be once the tool is viewed through the lens of ongoing business operations. For example, integrated reporting requires that organizations report on different types of information expanding upon traditional financial metrics and tools, but organizing the sheer volume of data can be a challenge.

The upside, however, is that many organizations already have internal reports, dashboards, and metrics to track and monitor operational performance in certain areas. Even if, traditionally, external shareholders and stakeholders were not particularly interested in the mechanics of how operations function, internal professionals most certainly were. The primary value add of artificial intelligence is not the technology itself, nor the technical underpinnings of how these platforms work, but the implications of what this tool will change for business management. A driving benefit of these changes is that management professionals, even if they do not understand the technical specifics of how the technology works, can leverage this tool to analyze and communicate data in a more continuous format. Linking this ability, the capability to process information and report it from a variety of different sources on an almost continuous basis to the multiple capital model is a logical next step in the discussion surrounding artificial intelligence. Creating a template to communicate the different types of information and data is an excellent start, but in order to generate a true value added method of communicating information, this template has to be populated.

To produce consistently the different types of capital embedded within an integrated report, management must be able to harness and process the underlying data. Environmental information, data on employee training and development, corporate governance issues, and connecting the investments made in plant, property, and equipment to continued business success are critical factors in determining the sustainability of business success, specifically whether or not the organization is sacrificing long term success for short term results. Leveraging these flows of information and data, including the ability of management to both understand internally and communicate effectively to external partners, forms the basis of how integrated reporting will influence management decision-making. Artificial intelligence tools and platforms, the specifics of which will inevitably change over time, will only have an increasingly large part to play in the reporting and analysis of information.

Blockchain Technology

For our discussion around the topic of integrated reporting, getting this definition correct is important. With all of the buzz and coverage around blockchain technology there is the potential for a muddled definition, which then makes arguing for investment in this technology difficult.

Working definition: The most appropriate definition appears to focus around the distributed ledger technology aspect of blockchain, meaning that information entered and uploaded into an organization is accessible in real time by all members having joined the network.

One of the critical gaps in the link between information being generated by an organization, the processing and control of data, and the communication of this information to external stakeholders is the possibility that these data will be stolen and hacked by malicious organizations and other third parties. Blockchain technology, at the essence of the technology tool, is a platform and methodology that allows the transparent and real-time transmission of information on a continuous basis. Applicable and useful for both financial and nonfinancial information, at the core of the platform is the idea that once information is compiled and added to the blockchain itself the blocks of data form a virtually immutable record comprising a, to date, tamperproof store of data. As different information is uploaded onto the blockchain, verified, and certified by the utilization of both public keys and private keys of the parties involved, it forms the block component of the blockchain. These blocks, which may consist of financial and operational information, are also assigned a unique ID name of letters and numbers associated with the information contained with the block.

Before the transactional information, consisted and composed in the block to be uploaded and added to existing blocks, is added to the blockchain, the information and block itself must be verified and approved by all existing members of the current blockchain. Even more appropriate for organizations seeking to join and develop a blockchain, it is free and easily accessible for organizations to download, join, and become part of the various blockchain networks and functionalities. Since all data must be verified and approved by existing members, including an option by which 51% of all current members of the chain must approve the addition of any data into the blockchain, it helps ensure that the consensus approval process is valid in nature. Additionally, and representing another safeguard against potential fraud and unethical activity, is the power requirements necessary to compute, approve, and add information to the blockchain environment. Organizations must invest in technology assets including both servers and personnel, as well as contending with the increased electricity costs necessary to manage and effectively use the blockchain platform.

Connecting blockchain to integrated reporting is a logical extension of both the increased integration of technology in the business decision-making process, and the increased interest of stakeholders in obtaining more comprehensive information linked to organizational performance. While certain public blockchains, namely the public (also known as permissionless) blockchain underpinning Bitcoin, have received the majority of coverage and analysis, there is an option in the blockchain environment that may actually generate increased benefits for specific organizations and institutions. One of the other key attributes of the blockchain environment, in addition to the security and confidentiality created within this environment is the real-time and continuous nature by which these data are available to participants within the blockchain. While public blockchains are, clearly, a step forward in both increased data security and communicating information to stakeholder groups, the concept of a private blockchain may actually be a simpler and more logical place to begin this implementation.

Private Blockchains

Blockchain technology may represent a step forward in the technological landscape and attract the attention of a number of stakeholder groups, but even though enhanced security and encryption is a component of this platform, public blockchains may not be an ideal fit for every organization. Private blockchains, conversely, appear to combine the benefits of encryption and security, while also limiting potential exposure and cost obligations to a limited number of organizations. Specifically, a private blockchain is mainly equivalent to the idea of a walled garden as it pertains to data and information management, namely the fact that a limited number of organizations and stakeholders participate in the verification and communication of information. This does limit the transparency aspect of blockchain, since only a limited number of participants are involved in this situation, but also creates an environment where specific stakeholders do have access to information in a real-time manner. Applying this scenario to situations that often face the management, namely the pressure brought to bear by activist investors on the management team unveils potential for future implementation.

Looking further, the intersection of a private blockchain with an integrated reporting framework continues to emerge and become clear. A key aspect and benefit of an integrated reporting framework and model is that data are distributed and accessible to all members of the blockchain. For example, instead of having to contend with periodic calls and meetings with stakeholder groups, management professionals would be able to distribute and report information to stakeholder groups about changes at the organization and all related data. Improving communication and distributing the flow of data, especially between organizations, supply chain partners, and external users of organizational data will facilitate the strategic planning and implementation process.

For example, private blockchains are already in use by organizations such as Wal-Mart, Toyota, and General Electric. Clearly worth noting at this point, is that many of the use cases and implementation cases currently in the market apply to some of the largest organizations doing business on a global basis. Due to resource constraints, namely the cost of installing the necessary hardware, hiring appropriate personnel, and establishing an appropriate electrical infrastructure, blockchain will inevitably be adopted initially by some of the larger organizations. That said, one of the most significant business benefits and upsides for blockchain technology, especially in a global business environment, are the implications it will have on supply sourcing and the verification of data throughout the chain. Drilling down specifically, some of the upsides and connections to integrated reporting can be illustrated through the example below.

Supply Chain Blockchain

One of the most applicable benefits, as it pertains to integrated reporting and facilitating buy-in amongst management professionals and organizations, is the real-time nature of information. Instead of pinging suppliers and partners with emails or other types of messages, all organizations belonging to the private blockchain can, at any time, examine transactions records to ascertain where certain inventory or other items are at any time during the shipping process. While certain amounts of information are currently available via the use of RFID tags and communication tools, having access to this information in a continuous manner reduces friction and lag in accessing these data. Even if the information, as it often is, is available to different stakeholder groups, compatibility issues and problems can hamstring these current attempts to get information in a real-time manner. Blockchain, especially a private blockchain that consists of an organization and its supply chain partners, facilitates the transfer of information between different organizations even if different enterprise resource programs are utilized. Connecting this concept and idea, which seems primarily like a technological upgrade, to the implementation and adoption of integrated financial reporting is an important step toward the intersection of technology and enhanced reporting capabilities.

For example, an underlying concept and driving force of integrated reporting is that the management team is able to facilitate the delivery of information to stakeholder groups in a continuous and verifiable manner. Especially as it links to supply chain issues and the host of human rights and environmental issues often embedded within that analysis, it is arguably more important than ever for management professionals to access this information and rely on the veracity of data. Integrated reporting encourages the delivery and communication of different types of information and data, but securing this information is a critical first step in maintaining control over the dissemination of information. Organizational data, including sustainability, environmental, and operational information can also be embedded within the blockchain environment.

Whether the specific organization is dealing with natural resources, food and food related items, potential conflict minerals, obtaining goods from global supply partners, tracking and verifying the provenance of these goods is paramount. Not only do these issues matter from a strictly financial and operational perspective, but they can also help limit potential legal liability and exposure to hidden risks down the road. Even more telling, since any type of information can be uploaded and included onto the blockchain platform, this information can include real-time temperature and location data. While such information will inevitably help in managing business on a continuous basis it can also help track and pinpoint problems.

Operational benefits and efficiencies related to supply chain blockchain are perhaps the clearest place to begin the implementation and analysis of blockchain in a business context. A relatively basic example of the intersection between operations, blockchain, and integrated reporting could play out as follows. Once a private blockchain has been established and members added, verified, and approved, information and data of virtually every kind is now available to participants in a real-time manner. A port management firm, receiving real-time updates and having access to both internal and supplier information can more effectively deploy resources and personnel. While this may appear similar to current information availability, the key differentiator is that the friction in these processes has been either eliminated or greatly reduced. Since all participants, including both the management of the port organization and the supplier shipping the goods have access to data as a result of belonging to the blockchain itself, there is no need for delays or mishaps in the communication and distribution of this information.

Blockchain Applications and Integrated Reporting

Blockchain may seem like a promising technology tool and platform, and from all evidence to date it appears to hold quite a bit of potential for businesses in the marketplace, but one fact is important to remember when connecting this trend to integrated reporting. Integrated reporting, after all, generates and promotes increased transparency and access to a broader array of information, and not just financial information. This connects directly to the potential and upside of blockchain technology—often thought of a financial platform, which is in fact a data management system that can be used to store, access, and analyze information of virtually any type. It is also worth noting that while, at this time the majority of implementation and development is occurring at the largest organizations, as increased investment occurs in this arena, cost savings and increased user friendliness is all but inevitable. Acknowledging this reality, however, does not represent a comprehensive analysis of the situation or connect this technology platform to the idea of integrated reporting. This connection, which may not appear clear at first glance, is profound and important to understand.

One of the most important aspects of integrated reporting is communicating these different types of information to different stakeholders, and this is where the value of blockchain to integrated reporting becomes more apparent. Specifically, the different types of information contained in a private blockchain environment, which can be thought of as a network like any other private network, allow all members of the network to access information on a continuous basis. This might seem like a marginal change or an alteration directly linked to data processing and interpretation of that information, but this is an action-oriented item that facilitates integrated reporting and the value it creates. Allowing information to be distributed in a real-time and continuous manner means that stakeholders can initiate an ongoing dialogue regarding the direction and performance of the organization. Reducing this friction, particularly as it relates to communicating information and the strategy built off of this information is an important part of how organizations can leverage integrated reporting to advance their objectives.

Integrated Reporting in a Frictionless Environment

Integrated reporting, at a basic and underlying level, embodies the idea that in order to effectively manage organizations and create growth over a spectrum of time frames, a variety of information must be consulted and utilized. Gathering this information, as noted throughout this text, requires effort, investment, and personnel on the side of the organization itself, but also requires a reduction in communication friction. In the context of business, business management, and making effective organizational choices friction exists in virtually every interaction in both the internal and external environment. Especially in the context of a globalized business environment where decisions can, and often are, increasingly automated and digitized in nature, delays and frictions in communicating information and data between different stakeholder groups can harm organizational performance. One rising specific business tool and application that incorporates both blockchain and integrated reporting options is the smart contract across business lines.

Smart Contracts and Integrated Reporting

Blockchain technology and the various platforms supported by a host of actors in the marketplace aim to, in addition to the other benefits and attributes associated with the technology, reduce friction and delays in communicating information. Smart contracts, which are digitally uploaded and secured by the blockchain technology itself, can assist not only with business operations but can also help ensure supply chain compliance as well. Conflict minerals, environmental issues, human rights concerns, and labor law violations are matters of concern and management attention across industry lines. Automating both the terms and conditions of agreement between firms and stakeholder groups, in addition to reducing costs linked to compliance and enforcement, also helps ensure compliance with regulatory terms and conditions. Digitizing and automating terms and conditions associated with both the requirements of parties in contracts and the associated benefits also reduce some of the costs and business friction often associated with contractual negotiations. Integrated reporting requires that information and data be communicated to stakeholders in a timely manner, and also that associated stakeholders achieve both buy-in, and are aware of the strategic plan put into place by management professionals.

The automation and digitization of contracts, contractual terms, and the associated rights and obligations are increasingly important in a stakeholder-oriented environment. Stakeholders, both financial and nonfinancial in nature, are interested in how an organization is performing now and in the future. Subsequent events, undisclosed liabilities, and the implications that these changes to the business environment can have on the organization in the future are important from both a financial and operational perspective. Financial implications of subsequent events, and undisclosed liabilities associated with these subsequent events, such as those at BP and Volkswagen, generate financial, legal, and operational issues for both the organization and the associated management teams. Clearer communication, more proactive governance, and increased transparency on the parts of these organizations would not have prevented such unethical activity, but possibly would have assisted in communicating about this information up front.

Data Analytics

At first glance the connection between a quantitative and data-driven competency and skill set, such as data analysis and reporting, and a strategic concept such as integrated reporting may seem tenuous. This perception, however, is an incomplete view of both the concept and idea of analytics, as well as a lack of recognition of the implications of integrated financial reporting. At the core of the idea, data analytics and improving the analyses performed by management professionals at an organization are directly tied to the two following factors. First, management teams and specialists must have access to pertinent data streams and sources in order to conduct comprehensive reviews. Integrated reporting, by default, requires that organizations be driven and managed by a variety of information and data, including financial and nonfinancial information. Making effective decisions requires both the availability of information and the capability of management teams and professionals to analyze and make effective use of it.

Second, when building the bridge between pure quantitative analysis and the strategic planning process, the underlying reality becomes readily apparent. Regardless of how strategy and strategic planning information are communicated, whether in the form of dashboards, engagement with different stakeholder groups, or via social media channels, making effective decisions requires quantitative information. The specific channels of information will be different, obviously, depending on the organization in question, but data drive decision-making and integrated reporting provides a platform for more comprehensive data collection and analysis. Prior to looking into some examples of internal and external benefits that can be, and often are, associated with data analytics and reporting, the following point is imperative to understand: even if the organization has massive amounts of information available to analyze and to project decisions upon, linking it to the strategic planning and multiple capital model is necessary for the successful adoption and implementation of this process.

Connecting the multiple capital model and associated framework with both the broader implications of integrated reporting and the underlying technology tools available to assist with data analytics reveals the following points of commonality. First, since organizations are already gathering larger amounts of information, and doing so from a broader array of inputs, developing metrics and benchmarks for multiple capitals is an obvious development. For example, if an organization is already making investments in obtaining increased information with relation to supply chain operations, inventory levels, and capital investment, this facilitates the development of a capital framework in the area of manufactured capital. Additionally, if management is proactively engaged in the development, training, and retention of employees, such activity generates both internal and external benefits. Internally, improved retention and enhanced employee training and development improve both the morale of current employees and creates an organization that might achieve the coveted label of employer-of-choice in a specific market. Externally, and of interest to external financial stakeholders, if an organization is experiencing lower turnover and retraining rates the bottom line benefits are clear.

Data-Based Decision-Making

Integrated reporting, nonfinancial frameworks, and the greater intersection of technology and finance continue to demonstrate the importance and necessity of integrating quantitative information into the decision-making process. Data and other quantitative information have always played a prominent role in how projects are evaluated, initiatives are ranked, and how the strategy of the organization is drawn up; however, it appears the business environment is entering an new age of digital decision-making. Faced with this evolving business environment, reporting and the methods by which information should be communicated must also evolve and change as well. Integrated reporting, while not unusual or unique in the integration of information into how decisions are made, takes the next step by incorporating information from a variety of different sources into the evaluation and assessment of organizational performance. Whether taken into account and viewed from an internal or external perspective, fundamental changes to how business is managed, evaluated, and developed are evident.

One underlying truth and fact underpinning the development, adoption, and implementation of integrated reporting is the desire for more information and a greater variety of information than previously possible. Harnessing this desire and expectation of the marketplace, augmented by tools, sensors, and systems available to management professionals, creates an environment conducive for an expansion of quantitative metrics. Such an expansion is logical and reasonable in the marketplace for a variety of reasons, including that operational and other nonfinancial information are the pieces of information that drive the financial performance of the organization. Specifically, and equally of interest to financial and nonfinancial stakeholders is the manner by which financial metrics and results are produced by the organization. Against the backdrop of financial crises, failures of corporate governance, and a lack of sustainable business operations, access to more information, and access that in a continuous manner should be able to improve the transparency associated with the business decision-making process.

It is true that certain technology tools such as artificial intelligence, various blockchain applications, and increased data analytics will assist in the collection and analysis of organizational information, however, simply collecting this information for internal purposes is insufficient. Communicating these larger amounts of information to stakeholder groups, doing so in a transparent manner, and keeping stakeholders informed of changes to the broader business environment of the organization enables more up-to-date decision-making, as well as decisions that incorporate both short-term and longer-term optics. Making decisions underpinned by information, both operational and financial in nature, is a logical tactic to embrace in a business environment and landscape dependent on information from a virtually unlimited number of sources. Data, however, must be cleaned, analyzed, quantified, and formatted in such a way that makes it useful for decision-making, and not just analytical purposes. This discipline, and the creation of different types of capital embedded within the integrated reporting framework means that organizations and associated management professionals must utilize said information to make effective decisions.

Chapter 11

The Future of Integrated Reporting

Like any new idea, concept, reporting structure, or framework it is virtually impossible to accurately project or forecast the ultimate end state of how these trends eventually will play out. That said, and taking into account the growing interest in nonfinancial and other operational information, it does appear that this shift toward more comprehensive reporting of data does not represent a short-term trend of fixation. Rather, as global competition and intersection continues to increase across geographic and industry lines, the demand and interest in analyzing the performance of an organization from a more comprehensive perspective is not only important, but increasingly expected of management professionals. The future trends toward sustainable information, operational data, and building a bridge between financial and nonfinancial performance appear to only be increasing in importance as the globalized nature of business exercises a larger influence on the business decision-making process. Chapter 11, emphasizing the importance of how these trends will manifest themselves over time and in an iterative process, outlines possible future directions and applications for integrated reporting, which are applicable across industry lines.

Future Directions of Integrated Reporting

If anything is clear after conducting a review of the integrated reporting environment, or completing the reading of this text, it should be that the following realties are true and increasingly self-evident. First, in a global business environment increasingly driven by digitized and nonfinancial information, on top of traditional flows of financial data and reporting, a more comprehensive method for reporting information is a necessity. Public support for a more holistic and comprehensive methodology for reporting organizational performance runs the gamut from institutional investors to environmental stakeholder groups. Blackrock, the largest asset management on a global scale, with an excess of $6 trillion in assets under management, published and supported in 2017 and 2018 a redefined view on just how organizations should operate. In essence, the underlying message of this campaign is to emphasize the importance of not only achieving and reporting financial information, but to also analyze, quantify, and report nonfinancial information in a holistic manner. Regardless of the specific stakeholder informational request and motivation for encouraging a more comprehensive view of this framework, the pursuit of a more robust framework and model is clear across geographic boundaries.

On top of the influence and motivation for different stakeholder groups, there are other less evident, but equally important financial shareholders also driving the adoption and changes toward a more comprehensive reporting framework. Specifically, pensions and endowments represent trillions of dollars in investable assets, often have board seats and directorships at a variety of larger organizations, and employ teams of experts to analyze and differentiate investing options. Interestingly, and importantly for the context of this research and analysis, is the fact that the underlying support for a more comprehensive reporting structure is not as important as the support itself. Especially in the context of college/university endowments, the returns generated by investments must both fulfill financial requirements and expectations and be sustainable over the medium and long term. This is also an appropriate place to revisit, one more time, the importance of sustainability in the context of environmental concerns and the ability of the organization to generate said returns over different periods of time.

Accounting professionals, management experts and advisors, and the accounting profession at large are simultaneously proponents of a more comprehensive framework and possess the capability to do so. Existing competencies and skill sets, including the reporting and explanation of quantitative information to internal and external end users, are equally applicable to an environment conducive to integrated reporting. As management teams and organizations come into possession of ever-increasing amounts and types of information, the need and requirements for analytics, dashboards, and reports linked to these different types of information will only grow. Additionally, the accounting profession is also well positioned to benefit from the greater automation and digitization of information, and not just from the increased quantification of information. As increased amounts of data and entry level accounting work are automated and taken over by technology platforms, accounting professionals and the industry as a whole has more time and flexibility for higher-level decision-making.

The connection between integrated reporting and the increased adoption of integrated reporting across different industry lines may seem like a minor issue, or a tangential topic, but these linkages and connections are critically important.

Historically, one of the largest challenges to market adoption and stakeholder interest in developing nonfinancial reporting and information was a lack of standards and consistency. Management professionals, regardless of industry or geographic location, require and increasingly expect information that is consistent, comparable, and analyzable over periods of time. Financial information, as governed by the current accounting and attestation frameworks, fulfill these expectations and are tested periodically by external accounting professionals. Looping in the accounting profession, specifically the attestation and auditing branches of the profession, is a step that must be solidified if the adoption of integrated reporting is to succeed. Put simply, there is only so much governmental mandate or stakeholder pressure can lead to in terms of integrated reporting adoption.

Stakeholder interest, even when it takes the form of large financial investors, only creates an appropriate environment and landscape for increased management buy-in and support, but does not construct a framework or methodology to translate this interest into reality. The multiple capital model, in an important differentiation from previous nonfinancial reporting frameworks, provides a quantitative platform for communicating these data. Incorporating the six types of capital into reporting and delivering information to different stakeholder groups is a key component of the value created via the utilization of an integrated reporting framework. Interestingly, and critically important for the connection of integrated reporting to other business trends and forums, by utilizing a multiple capital framework management professionals can connect these trends and information to other trends in the marketplace.

Integrated Reporting and Other Emerging Areas

No change occurs in a vacuum, and the development and increased adoption of integrated reporting is not an exception. Even with the buy-in and support provided by financial institutions and the accounting profession, it is important to acknowledge and recognize that other forces are creating a market receptive to such changes. Sustainability, namely, is a major driving force in the adoption and implementation of a more robust and comprehensive view of organizational performance, and is a recurring theme among stakeholders across geographic and industry boundaries. Building on the prior history and track record, reporting sustainability information on a consistent basis provides a solid foundation from which to develop a multiple capital framework inclusive of comprehensive streams of information. Environmental sustainability has been a growing force of reporting and data analytics in the industry landscape, but has recently taken a slightly different turn and approach than previously. Namely, the focus has shifted from exclusively reporting on environmental matters to connecting these environmental forces and information to the financial results and performance achieved by an organization. Mirroring the evolution of the business landscape along these lines, there is also clear support and connections between integrated reporting and other market initiatives oriented toward more comprehensive and holistic reporting programs. Specifically, and linking back to the multiple capital model and information contained therein, several areas of connection and commonality become evident.

Sustainability, clearly, is an area of market analysis and focus that is of importance for both management professionals and an idea that forms a core component of integrated reporting. Natural capital is a quantification of sustainability initiatives and projects underway at an organization and provides management leaders a method to communicate this information to the marketplace. This step forward, improving the information delivery systems and methods linked to sustainability data, does indeed differentiate integrated reporting from other sustainability oriented reporting frameworks. Operating in an environmentally oriented and sustainable manner appears to be good not only for the bottom line of the organization from a financial perspective, but for the ability of the firm to generate said returns over the medium and long term. Even more profound, however, is the linkage and connection of integrated reporting and the ideas and concepts of human capital.

Human capital is a critically important idea when it comes to both establishing a long-term value creation platform and facilitating the adoption and implementation of a more comprehensive reporting platform. Put simply, this connection and linkage is apparent simply due to the fact that corporations must invest in the training, development, and education to keep pace in the market. Technology, namely enhanced data analytics, blockchain technology, and the increasing integration of artificial intelligence into the business decision-making process provides both numerous opportunities but also represents a challenge for management professionals across industry lines. Training and investment in the development of employees is no longer an optional investment or technique that can be delegated as a lower level function or tactic—it is a necessity in the global business landscape. Integrated reporting connects to this trend and force as well, in the shape and form of intellectual and human capital, both of which require an investment in technology tools and in the employees that will utilize said tools.

Generating sustainable returns and incorporating the broader forces of the marketplace driving the need for a more comprehensive system of reporting and communication is the fiduciary duty of every management team across the globe. This is not a radical concept, clearly, but it is one worth reiterating in the context of integrated reporting and analyzing the returns generated therein. Short termism, misallocation of capital, and the underinvestment in long-term capital assets, management may, inadvertently or on purpose, artificially increase returns and financial performance in the short term, but starve the organization of capital, investment, and employee development so critical for success. Fiduciary duty should not just mean the returns that are reported on a quarterly basis to financial shareholders, but should also take into account the growth, strategic initiatives, and development of broad-based business lines. Integrated reporting appears to address this current gap in the landscape, by providing a framework to address a need in the marketplace. Put simply, current reporting and disclosure frameworks do not successfully address the needs of stakeholders, both internal and external.

Implementation

Implementing such a reporting framework, which will invariably involve substantive changes to both internal processes and external communications, may seem intimidating and outright daunting given the sheer scope of informational changes necessary to adapt to a rapidly changing environment. Faced with the numerous disruptions driven by technology and stakeholder-oriented business plans, organizations may simply place the implementation of an integrated reporting framework on the proverbial back burner. This, while seemingly a short-term solution that produces cost savings and pushes off the issue to a future date, will leave the organization and management teams unprepared to effectively deal with and navigate a rapidly changing business environment. While this list of suggested steps and recommendations below is not exhaustive, or serves as the only possible route forward, it does leverage existing information and guidance to assemble a logical succession of steps toward full adoption.

Clearly, every organization will be different, is going to face individual issues and pressures, and the regulatory forces in place will be distinct, but several fundamental tactics can be applied across industry lines. Assembling an action-oriented plan and a succession of steps represents the best fundamental way any organization can take to analyze integrated reporting and reap its associated benefits.

1. Conduct an assessment of current reporting trends among competitors, and leverage publicly available resources such as the information, categorization, rankings and listings published by organizations that include the IIRC, SASB, AICPA, and IMA. In addition to conducting a review and assessment, however, organizational leadership must also document and outline shortcomings in current reporting. It is important to recognize that current paint points may be identified with reporting delivered to internal stakeholders and external stakeholders. These shortcomings, or rather, opportunities for improvement, may include the following issues:
   a. Lack of timeliness in reporting, which is a common issue as it pertains to reporting audited financial information to financial markets.
   b. Too narrow a focus on financial information, without a clear indication of how these results are generated, or the implications of current performance on the long-term health and viability of the organization.
   c. Reporting of nonfinancial information, but doing so in an inconsistent manner that makes comparisons and updating difficult.
   d. Excessive amounts of ad hoc reporting, which can all too often result in information, templates, and reports created for different end users that contain different information, without a uniform approach or delivery method.

2. Understand what types of information are available to management with current reporting and analytics tools. This can be an overlooked point that inadvertently causes organizations to purchase or invest in technology tools that not only are not needed, but do not add much in terms of value. Especially in a competitive business environment, where every percentage point of profitability is closely scrutinized, being sure to exercise fiduciarily aligned conservatism with regards to expenditures is essential. Drilling down, some of the questions that should be asked by management include, but are not limited to the following:

   a. What reporting and data collection systems does the organization already have in place within the firm to optimize information collection and reporting? Specifically, most every organization will surely have operational systems and platforms in place to continuously monitor and assess internal systems and performance. Taking advantage of this information can provide an organization with insights into how the bridge between operations and finance can be constructed.

   b. Are specific business divisions or geographic areas over or underperforming the rest of the organization in terms of efficiency or productivity? In either case, increased attention to these issues generates benefits:

      i. If there is one, or a handful of divisions outperforming the rest of entity, best practices, processes, and systems should be exported to the rest of the organization.

      ii. Conversely if one area of the division is underperforming, the insights from internal system analysis can be used to improve operations and results for this underperforming area.

3. Which area of the multiple capital model is of greatest interest or importance to the organization, which will be a different consideration and approach for every organization. In some instances, for example a mining or timber company, the connection between sustainability and natural capital is clear. That said, an approach that can be replicated across industry and geographic lines can include but is not limited to the following tactics and methods:

   a. Assess what types of nonfinancial information is of greatest interest to external stakeholders, including both financial and nonfinancial groups—and this will be different for different organizations—but similar approaches and questions can be used to ascertain this information. Perhaps most importantly is to understand some of the following points:

      i. Who are the major organizational stakeholders? This may seem like a relatively basic question to ask, but understanding just who major stakeholders are can make a definitive difference in how the reporting and communication processes of the organization are constructed. Like any conversation strategy it is imperative that management understand who the audience is when constructing the narrative.

    ii. Figure out what these different stakeholder groups are interested in, and wish to know more about? Clearly consumer groups are going to be interested in the products or services offered by an organization, but increasingly they are also interested in just how these products and services are produced. With 80 million members in the United States alone, and hundreds of millions more on a global basis, including several heads of state, the millennial generation's interest in sustainability and comprehensive reporting will be a force to be reckoned with for years to come.

4. Determine which stakeholders receive which information, how often this information is communicated to different stakeholder groups, and the format in which core stakeholder groups like to receive this information. This may seem like a throwaway mention or comment versus the operational complexity of actually implementing a new or more comprehensive framework, but it is important to understand what exactly this means for communication and data management. Especially in an environment where both financial and nonfinancial stakeholders continue to exercise larger amounts of influence over the decision-making process, taking into account what types of data matter most to what stakeholder groups is an important step in ensuring a smooth transition to a more comprehensive reporting framework. Drilling down specifically, several other considerations should be included in both how data are reported, and how often this more comprehensive view of organizational performance is communicated.

    a. Understand that, regardless of what specific information is preferred or communicated to different stakeholder groups, a baseline of consistent information should be distributed to all stakeholders, including a summary of both financial and operational data. Even if certain stakeholders, for example, are more interested in strictly financial outcomes and earnings will at least have some sort of interest in how these results have been achieved.

    b. What format is most appealing, interesting, or helpful to the stakeholder groups in question? Some recipients may be more interested in detailed statistical reports connected to operational efficiency and results, whereas other stakeholder groups may be more interested in the environmental impact of those same operations. Even more granular information may be of interest to consumer advocacy groups, regulators, or industry associations, which may include but will not be limited to customer feedback, service statistics, and engagement with the professional community.

    c. Figuring out what information should be communicated to the stakeholder community, which while important, is only one half of the equation. The second half of the equation should be how often this information can be reported and communicated to stakeholders using existing information and data management systems currently in place at the organization.

The preparation, analysis, and reporting of these different types of information will inevitably require management time, investment, and resources, so understanding how often these data streams can be put together forms the cornerstone of which information can be put together for external analysis.

5. Harness social media, which may have a less than stellar reputation in the current marketplace due to hacking and data scraping scandals; however, it is still a powerful tool that can, and should be, harnessed to help to both collect important organizational information and report these findings to the marketplace. Drilling down, the interactive nature of social media, whether it is via Twitter, Facebook, or other venues, provides a critical bridge between the actions taken by the management team, and market reactions to these actions. Taking feedback into account allows the organization to not only gauge current levels of interest and opinion, but to also possibly forecast future reactions and opinions. It is not enough, especially as social and relational capital are embedded within the multiple capital model, to simply have several employees working on different social media platforms. Drilling down to some of the benefits of social media, putting together a strategy around these areas begins to take shape:

a. Figure out what social media works best for your organization, which will vary both depending on the expertise available in house and the different stakeholder groups who will be receiving this information. For example, a consumer-based organization that deals in primarily a business-to-consumer business model will have greater levels of engagement with their end users, generally, than a firm dealing primarily with business clientele.

b. Put together a strategy for how to leverage social media for increased engagement, which may sound excessive but is important for organizations seeking to achieve the full benefits of a more proactive social media strategy. Like any other project, initiative, or investment, it's important to have a plan to maximize the effectiveness of resources and personnel that are dedicated to this initiative.

c. Track, evaluate, and analyze the effectiveness of social media engagement strategies both initially, in the medium term, and in response to different projects launched by the organization. Especially in such a reactive and stakeholder-based business environment, the reactions and feedback loop created by launching projects create a unique situation for management to respond continuously to market forces.

The Upside

Integrated reporting is, at the most basic form, a reporting framework and methodology that seeks to address several shortfalls in how information is current

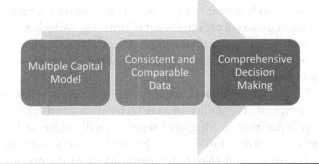

Figure 11.1   Illustrating the MCM for business decision-making.

reported, compiled, and disseminated to the marketplace. In order to sell and document the improvements, benefits, and costs associated with a new reporting and communicating framework, specific benefits must be outlined and documented for management analysis. Especially when attempting to implement, change, or augment current reporting standards, frameworks, and communication concepts it is essentially important to make sure that the benefits and upsides of integrated reported are communicated clearly to both internal or external stakeholders. Expanding on the upside and benefits of integrated reporting, in and of itself, is an excellent first step, but should also be augmented and reinforced by how integrated reporting improves the current reporting and information communication structure (Figure 11.1).

Illustrated by real-world implementation and applications included in this book by organizations that have implemented a full-fledged integrated financial reporting, and a robust discussion around the broader trends driving this adoption, it is important to also highlight the benefits of integrated reporting versus current standards. Financial reporting, which despite its upside, benefits, and quality of information communicated between organizations and stakeholder groups, does generate significant gaps and deficiencies that can be addressed with a comprehensive framework. Identifying the current gaps in financial reporting information and frameworks, and outlining how integrated reporting can help address these gaps, management professionals should begin the dialogue with regards to how, and in what phases, integrated reporting should be adopted within an organization.

Traditional financial reporting has several characteristics that make it increasingly unhelpful and almost obsolete in the current market environment.

Current Pain Point: Limited Scope

First, financial reporting is assembled with a narrow set of end users in mind, namely creditors and equity shareholders who are almost without exception primarily focused on the financial performance of the organization above all other data. This, however accurate it may appear from an initial analysis, only represents a partial view of just what end users of organizational information are looking for in reports. Increasingly, and including financial and nonfinancial stakeholders, end users are interested in not only the financial performance of the organization, but how that performance is generated.

Specifically, as stakeholders seek stability and earnings growth in an uncertain political environment, the ability of management to consistently deliver and grow earnings is paramount. Integrated reporting will not, in and of itself, cure an organization of financial difficulties, but will enable management to more comprehensively report and analyze the performance of the organization, from a financial and operational perspective. This more comprehensive approach also connects to another area of importance for organizations seeking to succeed and thrive in a digital environment—the need for continuous information and analysis.

Current Pain Point: Lack of Timeliness of Information Delivered to Market

Traditionally, financial statement information is prepared first by the management and internal accounting employees of the organization and audited by external accounting professionals on a periodic basis. This audit process, relying on sampling methods to project findings and opinions across the entirety of the financial statements, can also lead either to a lack of audit efficiency (with too many samples taken) or a failing of audit effectiveness (with material misstatements going unnoticed). In addition, the time this process currently takes can be months in duration and can generate a significant lag between when the information was generated, when it was collected and analyzed internally, and when it was ultimately communicated to external stakeholders.

While there are certain processes and applications that can assist auditors and organizations in uncovering subsequent events, and footnote requirements allowing the communication of important information, the multiple month lag can result in information, frankly, not being terribly useful for decision-making purposes. Technological advances, specifically the advances related to artificial intelligence, blockchain technology, and improved analytics tools allow both accounting professionals and management teams better access to more information in real time. Harnessing, quantifying, and reporting these multiple streams of data lies at the heart of the integrated reporting concept, specifically the multiple capital model.

The multiple capital model is a unique aspect of integrated reporting that helps to create several significant benefits for the organization. Perhaps most importantly, it allows the company and management team to report and communicate nonfinancial information in a manner consistent and familiar to how financial information is normally communicated. This approach may seem like a minor tweak or change in approach but, in fact, represents a fundamental shift in how nonfinancial information is communicated to stakeholder groups. This differentiation builds on two other problems and issues with reporting that consistently detract from the value delivered by financial statements. Even more important for nonfinancial information, creating a standardized framework and reporting framework for these data are critical to encourage adoption and implementation of an integrated reporting framework.

Current Pain Point: Lack of Comparability of Information

Comparability is a key function and feature of financial reporting and information of data to internal and external stakeholders, and one that is embedded into information communicated to market analysts and nonfinancial users. Financial information may be generated internally on a weekly or monthly basis, and is reported to the marketplace on at least a quarterly basis. This consistency and periodicity of information serves two purposes that allows management professionals to understand both what this information means and to compare the current results and performance to data generated in the future. Comparing the results of the organization is clearly a benefit for shareholders and nonfinancial stakeholders, which allows management and external shareholders to judge and navigate the organization moving forward in a competitive environment.

The comparability of financial information also allows these data and information to be applied across industry and geographic lines. For example, net income is a metric that is widely understood, discussed, and analyzed by management professionals and is also a metric that can be dissected and examined across industry lines. Comparability of information, both between past performance of the organization and the performance of peers and competitors, is a critical factor in understanding not only how the organization is performing, but also defining what are the possibilities of successfully moving forward. Nonfinancial information, however, has not traditionally been presented in a standardized format that is equivalent to financial information, which is something that can hamstring the implementation and adoption process.

A recurring example of how nonfinancial information is not presented on a consistent and comparable basis is the reality that, depending on industry and geographic region, different types of sustainability and nonfinancial information will be different. Clearly, there will be differences between the types of information that are most important to stakeholder and shareholder groups, but in order to move toward a globalized stakeholder-oriented environment some comparability is required. Integrated reporting, specifically the multiple capital model, requires that organizations adopt such a framework to organize, quantify, and report a wide array of information on a consistent basis. The specifics will differ from organization to organization, but the overarching idea of the multiple capital model is to connect as closely as possible the reporting of nonfinancial information and financial information to the methods with which financial information is reported. Connecting this framework, specifically the reporting of different types of information over time, is a definitive shift in how data are communicated and disseminated to end users.

Inconsistent Standards with Financial Information

Standards, regulation, and consistency with regard to how information is communicated to internal and external users of information forms the foundation of how accounting and financial information can be used across industry and geographic lines. Put simply, and regardless of whether the specific financial information is prepared and reported under a U.S. GAAP or IFRS reporting construct, many of the underlying fundamentals are similar. Especially as these standards increasingly converge on technical items such as valuation, intangible assets, and the reporting of certain investment items the differences embedded in different reporting frameworks continue to decrease. Taken at a high level, and especially contrasting with the wide array and variety of reporting options available for reporting nonfinancial information, the differences are stark. An example or analogy that can be used to illustrate just how different the reporting of financial and nonfinancial information continues to be is to imagine attempting to measure distance with one method of measurement, such as yards, and attempting to measure the same distance using a combination of yards, feet, kilometers, inches, and so on. The same information might be there, but it will take much longer and be much more difficult to eventually arrive at that conclusion. This, however, only represents on negative implication of this lack of standardized communication with regards to nonfinancial data.

If information or data are not governed by a consistent set of standards or metrics there is also a more insidious or negatively correlated possibility that may arise. In the vacuum that arises because of a lack of authoritative or governing standards, there is the distinct possibility that greenwashing and other superficial methods of reporting and communicating nonfinancial data will arise and enter the marketplace. Examples of this in past examples abound, including examples including food safety, environmental contamination and shortcomings, automobile manufactures attempting to circumvent regulations, and other examples, but this is does not encapsulate the totality of the situation. As business increasingly becomes globalized, digitized, and interconnected the implications of nonfinancial information and reporting will only become more important. Perhaps the most high profile example to illustrate this point is the simply reality that supply chains operate on a global basis, and this supply chain situation does not just pertain to the largest multinational organizations. Small to midsize organizations, many of which supply larger multinational organizations, also have suppliers, thus creating a network of interconnected businesses that can influence each other.

Stepping into this gap in the market are numerous organizations, some industry specific and some driven by professional associations, seeking to establish authoritative guidance and advice for reporting nonfinancial data and information. While these multiple options in the marketplace do provide much needed flexibility and industry-specific optionality, it is important to establish a baseline on how nonfinancial data can be reported, and how to connect these types of information to traditional financial information. Integrated reporting appears to offer a robust and comprehensive solution to this problem, although it will require accounting professionals and practitioners to adopt and evolve alongside the marketplace as a whole. This more leadership-oriented role for the profession may, at first glance, seem like a challenge for accounting professionals to contend with, but is in fact an opportunity for professionals with a proactive and forward-looking mindset.

Building out and implementing guidance that has already been developed and put into practice in various accounting associations provide a foundation from which proactive practitioners can develop implementation guidance and suggestions. Taking advantage of technology tools and platforms already present in the marketplace to help better analyze and examine information, generated from a variety of sources and information, will also assist the adoption and implementation process. Nonfinancial standards and frameworks, regardless of which association promotes and publishes the individual frameworks do have several commonalities, which should be acknowledged. First, the nonfinancial frameworks should mirror many of the techniques and strategies currently used for documenting and communicating financial information. Second, accounting professionals should use similar skills to those used for auditing, tax, assurance, and other reporting services, namely the interpretation of data into reporting templates and dashboards to help communicate the findings and insights generated from these different streams of information.

Selling Integrated Reporting to Management Professionals

At the core of the idea and concept of integrated reporting is the requirement that any change to reporting and communication of information adds value to the reporting process. In the current business landscape and backdrop, which is increasingly globalized and digitized, organizations must be able to justify and explain to internal and external stakeholders the value and value creation that integrated reporting offers to stakeholders. Especially as adopting integrated reporting (whether in steps, on a continuum, or on a larger scale) requires investments in both technology and personnel, the cost-benefit analysis of

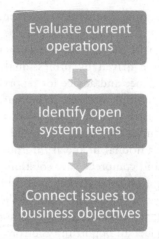

Figure 11.2   Marketing IR to management professionals.

integrated reporting must be constructed, narrated, and explained to employees, management professionals, and external stakeholders. Taking a step back and viewing the concept of integrated reporting from a higher-level perspective, and not just a reporting and compliance idea, illustrates a core idea of integrated reporting. The idea of integrated reporting is not a reporting framework, concept, or idea; it is much more and more expansive than yet any other reporting framework. Rather, it is an idea and concept that requires management to meet a variety of informational goals while also managing the business in a way that elevates both short and long-term value creation. Despite the words and pressures from different stakeholder groups, an overt focus on short-term profits and results has led management professionals to make decisions that are not optimal for either financial or nonfinancial stakeholders (Figure 11.2).

Connecting these concepts, the development of short-term value creation, including but not limited to quarterly earnings releases, with the longer-term goals of sustainable value generation put forward by stakeholders, is a difficult but not impossible task. What has often been lacking, however, is a consistent framework and methodology that will allow management professionals and organizations to report information related to a more comprehensive view of performance on a continuous basis. While there are multiple frameworks including those issued by the SASB, the IIRC, and guidelines communicated by the AICPA and IMA, this variety of frameworks may, in fact, increase confusion and miscommunication as it relates to information. The lack of standardized guidelines creates a situation where nonfinancial information is not communicated on a comparable or consistent basis, which in turn will detract from the value of this nonfinancial information. While not creating a situation where this issue is solved or an instance where organizations will inevitably begin operating in a sustainable manner, integrated reporting does provide a path forward.

Connecting the value of the organization, whether referenced via the increasingly value of intangible assets and information, or the market value of the organization in the marketplace to the reporting framework, is an important first step toward successful adoption and implementation of integrated reporting. Since market valuation is already a metric and tool used by external stakeholders to value and judge the performance of the organization, it is logical to continue using this tool. While it is true that market valuation, including but not limited to the price targets and market capitalization levels cited consistently on networks such as CNBC and Bloomberg, attract large amounts of market coverage and attention and can vary wildly from day to day, management professionals should pay attention to the impact integrated reporting will have on the performance of an organization moving forward.

Another angle that is important to emphasize and illustrate, as integrated reporting becomes a part of broader business conversation is that both internal and external stakeholders are equally as likely to be interested in a more holistic view of organizational performance. Operational information and data are what ultimately drive bottom line performance—but that is not the only reason why nonfinancial data are of increasing importance. As millennials begin to comprise ever-larger percentages and components of the population and workplace in general, the reporting and focus on nonfinancial information can also serve as a recruitment and retention tool. Attracting the best talent, retaining it, and developing capabilities to compete moving forward is part of the fiduciary duty every management team must follow and comply with. Highlighting the forward-looking nature and perspective of the organization and management team not only serves a functional role, by promoting the communication of performance, but also provides management with a potential recruiting tool.

Concluding Thoughts

Integrated reporting represents, instead of a brand new initiative or reporting paradigm, an iteration and evolution of existing reporting frameworks and constructs connected to nonfinancial information and data. Reporting information, regardless of the specific framework utilized by the organization, or within which industry the organization operates, forms an important part and aspect of the fiduciary duty of management teams; however, it does not in and of itself solve the problems embedded within the current reporting framework. Data, in numerous practitioner and academic publications, appear to form the competitive advantage that will continue to differentiate organizations from their competitors in the marketplace; it is a responsibility of management teams to acknowledge this reality. Information is what drives strategy, strategic planning, and long-term decision-making even if the narrative and structure around the decision-making process is qualitative in nature. Even in a digitally based environment, a globalized business landscape, and a competitive field driven by information and data, the ability to explain, justify, and narrate the decisions made by an organization is critically important.

Accounting professionals, already equipped with competencies and skill sets to analyze, report, and document the information generated and embedded within the organization, appear uniquely well positioned to assist with this evolution and process. Dashboards, templates, and reporting frameworks are how organizations and management professionals communicate the results and performance of the firm in the short, medium, and long term. Although much of the information generated by organizations, whether it is from operations, stakeholder-oriented activities, or other internal actions must be quantified and standardized, the fact is that organizations must be able to illustrate and highlight the performance of the firm moving forward. That said, it is not only accounting professionals that should be tasked with implementing an integrated reporting framework; such a wholesale transition requires input and services from a variety of organizations. In order to successfully implement the specifics of integrated reporting, this initiative and strategic shift must incorporate input and expertise from a variety of stakeholder groups.

The reality is, and this is evident from any analysis of market headlines, analyst coverage, or financial examination that organizations are increasingly being judged using a variety of metrics. Metrics that include, but are most certainly limited to financial information and results are critical to effective decision-making; management professionals must be able to keep pace with this changing reporting environment. No reporting framework, whether it is integrated reporting or some other option, is going to add value, improve customer service, or lead to investor satisfaction by itself. In order to add value a communicative framework must be supported by comprehensive changes to the business model of the organization. Integrated reporting, regardless of the industry or organization this reporting framework is applied to, virtually require changes to how information is processed, analyzed, and reported to internal or external users.

Making these changes, which have been analyzed and examined throughout this book, are neither simple to implement nor items that can be put into effect in a haphazard manner. Rather, and in order to reap the full benefits of an integrated reporting framework, the internal procedures changes must be phased in over time with buy-in from all involved stakeholders, which can take more or less time depending on organizational dynamics. As difficult as internal changes may be, however, the external changes and explanations that must accompany a shift in information can arguably be more difficult. Leveraging the accounting profession, building on examples of successful implementations in the marketplace covered in this book, and taking cue from leading firms in the market all represent logical starting steps. The beginning of this process is arguably the most important, as the trend toward more comprehensive reporting does not appear to be a fad or short-term trend. Building business for the medium and long term, engaging with stakeholders in a proactive and forward-looking manner, and incorporating the needs of different stakeholder groups into the conversation represent good business practices. Integrated reporting may not be the magic solution, or even the final iteration of more robust reporting and information communication, but it is an excellent first step.

The time to start is now.

Index

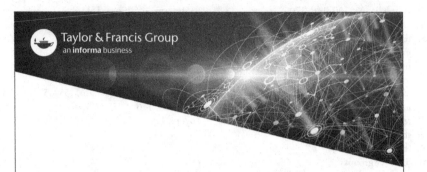

Printed in the United States
by Baker & Taylor Publisher Services